Women Who Lead

Timeless Life, Career, and Business Secrets from Inspiring Women Around the World

Julienne Waters

Publishing History

Paperback Edition 1 / October 2021
ISBN: 978-1-7948-8534-9
Imprint: Lulu.com

Dedications

I would like to dedicate this book to Elliott, Jamileh, Vincent, Khaleya, and Mikhela, my precious children who came along on this journey with me. With deep gratitude to Steve Ahl, as my champion supporter. My parents, who gave me life and the challenges to grow through along with my five siblings, each in their personal journey to wholeness. Gay and Katie Hendricks, my dear friend Eldonna Edwards, the many persons along the way who believed in me and stood by me, and the many many clients I have learned from. Also, Kinsley Wong, who taught me the KLS, Kinsley LifeStyle, a road to personal freedom, showered the world with his smile, his joy of life, and self-created freedom.
~ Julienne Waters

To my husband, family and best friends, thank you for your continued love and support. To my team – Jess, Des and Michelle – you're the best! To Carly – you're a blessing and thank you for being there when I needed you to be. To my beloved Grandma, thank you for showing me the true meaning of being a legend. To Ba, Yaya and Tomel, Mommy loves you very much. To all the women who have the courage to say YES to yourself, you are the prize darling!
~ Dr. Izdihar Jamil, Ph.D.

I would like to dedicate this with love to my best friend Phil, who has always been there for me, and who has helped me through some really tough times.
~ Marcia Martin

Thank you to the many people who had stood for my leadership even when I didn't see myself as a leader. To my extraordinary children, thank you for being my partners in creating a world that works for everyone! Mom, I have been forever blessed and shaped by your servant leadership. Mom and Dad, no words could fully express my gratitude to both of you for being the source of my life and my capacity to love. The size of my heart is the direct result of your example! To my love, anything and everything at any time, always!
~ Amber Howard

Dedications

I've been through a lot, but I know that each day can bring miracles. With that sentiment in mind, I dedicate this book to those who are determined to find their way, whether it's business, career, life, parenting, self-esteem and on and on the list can go. But I also dedicate this book to my mother, who taught me to be strong, my ex who believed in me and still does, and my children (Amber and Luke) who have been my inspiration and fuel through the tough days and long nights.

~ **Angelica "Angie" Monet**

I want to thank Matt, my Soulmate, for supporting me in all my crazy dreams and loving me even on my bad days. I also want to thank my clients, you who have entrusted in me your greatest fears and desires. I've got your backs, my lovelies!

~ **Emmy Hernandez**

I want to thank my beloved parents Agustina and Jorge for their sacred love to me and life, they inspire me incessantly!. Special thank you to my beloved Husband Mark Cook for his faithful and impeccable Love and belief in me. I also would love to express my eternal gratitude to my ancestors who have, and are, guiding me on this Divine Journey!

~ **Gabby Puma**

I need to take a quick moment and thank my incredible husband Tyler for being the man of strength and compassion that he is, and for always believing in me and my dreams. To my many coaches and mentors in my life that have been a support, a sounding board, demanding accountability, and holding unwavering faith – I am forever grateful! Thank you!

~ **Jessica Fox**

I want to thank my mom for always being there to support me and inspiring me to fulfill my goal in life. She is my best friend and I hope to someday grow to be the confident and caring woman that she is.

~ **Madison Marshall**

I would like to dedicate this chapter to my mom, my dad, my sister, John Murphy, Kristyn Caetano, Matt Brauning, Adam Lewis Walker, Saleem Haider, and Dr. Izdihar Jamil. The *TEDx* Speaker journey would not have been possible without your unconditional love and support in making this a reality for me. You believed in me even when I did not believe in myself. Thank you for making me the woman I am today.

~ **Michelle Mehta**

Women Who Lead

This book is dedicated to my parents, for raising me to always see the best in everything.

~ **Monica Ward**

I wish to dedicate this article to the many heroes and warriors who have fought COVID-19 through an unseen but a relentless battle. Your patriotism, professionalism, and resilience have been inspiring. Thank you for giving me a very good lesson on how humanity can be translated in many beautiful, different ways.

~ **Nurfadhlina Mohd Sharef**

To all the women out there who deserve to love and be loved deeply. And to the men I've been in a relationship with; I'm grateful for our experience together, the good times, and even the painful breakups, as they all helped me evolve, learn to love, respect, and value myself, and finally create the Love Education Academy and my Lasting Love Method and help hundreds of women find love.

~ **Raeeka Yaghmai**

To my parents, who taught me to be resilient and never give up.

~ **Sara Ruda**

Book Reviews

Reviews for Julienne Waters

"An inspiring story of transformation. I highly regard the author's honesty and vulnerability."
~ Tarryn Miller, Microbiologist with Genome Editing, USA

"Reaching from a depth that only knows courage and resilience, Julienne shares her story that encourages and enlivens the reader forward, towards their own transformational inner journey."
~ Vicchi Oleski, Energy Intuitive and Transformation Guide, USA

"Julienne Waters has written a moving, strong, and powerful story briefly describing a couple the traumas of her childhood which forged her into the powerful and strong woman she is today. I was able to find myself feeling her anguish AND her strength. I highly recommend both reading her story and reaching out to Julienne Waters."
~ Sue Mandell, Licensed B.A.N.K. Trainer, NLP Certified Trainer, USA

Reviews for Izdihar Jamil

"A relatable story! A message that can empower and inspire anyone who reads it. Her desire to achieve what she set out to do is really remarkable. A character of a true leader."
-- Nor Suhir, #1 International Bestselling Author, stroke survivor, Certified Social Media Strategist, and a Business Coach – Singapore

"An empowering read for entrepreneurial women, especially with young children. Izdihar shares her incredible journey as a loving mother and successful business owner open-heartedly."
~ Melissa Desveaux, #1 Bestselling Author, Author Consultant – Sydney, Australia.

"Dr. Izdihar's chapter entitled 'Make A Decision' in the book *Women Who Lead* is a total game-changer for entrepreneurs who wish to scale their businesses to greater heights. I would highly recommend her practical tips for making decisions in their entrepreneurship journey."
~ Najmunnisa Abdul Kader, #1 International Best Selling Author, Publisher, Queen N Books – Singapore

Book Reviews

"The chapter on 'Making a Decision' was very insightful. I love the strategy of weaving the process and the rituals of decision-making together through the lens of childbirth and the experiences of early motherhood. It was an excellent read and very relatable, especially for women who are new mothers and desirous of having a successful business."
~ Dr. Caroline Alexis-Thomas, owner and CEO of Silk Cotton Wellness Lifestyle Centre – Bon Accord, Tobago

"I found Izdihar's chapter to be not only highly inspiring but a succinct delivery of highly motivational actions within the decision-making ritual. A very powerful resource tool for entrepreneurs."
~ Mary Wishart, Entrepreneur, Biohacker, and Motivational Wellness Coach – Darwin, Australia

"I was blown away at the inspiration packed into Izdihar's story! The advice from a fellow Mompreneur on how to have it all without burning yourself out. Also, giving every mama permission to mess up but stretch for goals. Every mama needs to read this book!"
~ Vandee Flake, CEO: True Freedom LLC – USA

"Dr. Jamil Has Done It Again!
This chapter, Dr. Jamil's latest masterpiece, is just as amazing as her previous works. She consistently delivers essential and timely information in an engaging way. Dr. Jamil always offers exact strategies we can use to reach the type of success she has experienced. Her commitment to excellence and empowering people to become experts in their field is admirable. Additionally, Dr. Jamil's ability to position her unique story and differentiating characteristics as strengths, then use them as her superpowers is inspiring. I am so thankful that Dr. Jamil shares her many gifts with the world. This chapter is one such gift."
~ Naomi Beverly, Entrepreneur and #1 International Bestselling Author – USA

Reviews for Marcia Martin

"A valuable method for how to consciously respond rather than unconsciously react in challenging situations."
~ Jack Canfield, Coauthor of *New York Times* bestselling *Chicken Soup for the Soul*® series, USA

"Powerful advice, tools, distinctions, and strategies that have been instrumental in helping me build my global organization."
> ~ Dame Doria Cordova, Ph.D. (Hon.), CEO/Owner, *Excellerated Business Schools / Money & You*, USA

"Timeless wisdom never dates, and Marcia not just embodies it with grace and humor but makes it pertinent in any life context! She's an Oracle and her words are pure balm for the aspiring Soul."
> ~ Jenni Parker Brown, CEO & Founder, *House of Preeminence Magazine,* France

"Marcia's wisdom is the 'instruction manual' we all desire to have in our lives. She lives it and embodies it and is a great model for leading from center."
> ~ Maria Simone, CEO & Founder, *ZenMoose Capital*, USA

"A must-read for all women who lead or who desire to lead!"
> ~ Connie Benjamin, International Speaker, Best Selling Author of *Women with Fire*, USA

Reviews for Amber Howard

"Rich in heartache and truth, Amber nails what it looks like to look yourself in the eye and say, 'Hey, I'm here to stay, and I've got this! '"
> ~ Cindy Gillies, Lifestylist, Canada

"An authentic and empowering road map to self-love and leadership. "
> ~ Heather Shapter, Executive Director, International Development Organization, Canada

Reviews for Angelica "Andie" Monet

"Andie Monet's 'Blow Up The Box' is an uplifting and inspirational story as she sheds light on the fact that no matter how many struggles life can bring, anyone has the option to still make life happen."
> ~ Natalie Nasca, Managing Member, Right Audience Events LLC – USA

"Andie Monet is that rare person who really cares about the business AND the business owners she consults with her 'Blow Up The Box' approach offers tools that even the most experienced entrepreneur can learn, appreciate, and adopt."
> ~ Virginia Bays, Director of Finance, San Diego Repertory Theatre – USA

Book Reviews

"What a great read! Andie Monet's 'Blow Up The Box' had me in tears in the beginning but was truly inspiring, with 10 gold nuggets of wisdom at the end."

~ Kevin Bratton, President, Paladins Inc, Natalie, Virginia – USA

Reviews for Gabby Puma

"This beautiful, introspective, and moving book offers a glimpse into Gaby's inspiring journey in becoming a kind and wise guide and coach to many. Her unique ability to weave ancient wisdom with modern realities offers poignant life lessons for living with intention and impact. "

~Maddy Kulkarni, global marketing leader, professor, and author of *Social Impact Marketing*

"Gaby's courageous story and powerful transformational journey was inspiring to read. It left me reflecting on my life, the life of my patient's and on the lives of my colleagues. Especially relevant to me is her statement 'Once we live in the freedom of forgiveness and truth, instead of judgement and falsehood, we shift from being the victim of our life to being the creator of our life'. Being stuck in what someone else has done to us yesterday or today, being afraid of what they may do tomorrow gives our power away. If we really want to be living a successful magical life, and be a stand for human dignity, then we should all read Gaby's courageous story, and follow her helpful lessons and words of wisdom"

~ Deborah Borne, MSW, MD, Director of Health Policy for People Experiencing Homelessness and Vulnerable Populations, San Francisco Department of Public Health, Energy Medicine Practitioner, Tarot Reader., USA

"This book is a gorgeous invitation to allow ourselves to be whole.

I opened up to a chapter, and I could not put the book down as I found myself pulled into Gaby's life story wanting to learn more. Her experience is palpable, and she offers us a very rich gift: one of letting go of past baggage, honoring our gifts, and stepping into our most empowering time of life. She embodies ancient wisdom and catalyzes modern-day transformation.

To be in her presence, her deeper knowing, and her soulful sharing is to take a front-row seat in the circle of women leading authentically today."

~ Françoise Everett, MS, Feminine Leadership & Lifestyle, Coach, Facilitator, Speaker, and Collaborative Author of Wholehearted Wonder Women 50 Plus: Courage, Confidence & Creativity at Any Age. Founder & CEO of ELLE Unleashed, a feminine leadership training, coaching, and facilitation company.

Review for Jessica Fox

"Jessica gives yet another inspiring story of how we as mothers are able to become so much more and be whatever we truly desire. In doing so. we become our children's role models. Loved the chapter as much as working with this amazing lady."

~ Des Denysschen, Bestselling Author & Master Coach, USA

Reviews for Madison Marshall

"A beautiful story of strength, passion, and bravery... This is the place where midwives are born!"

~ Rachael Herrera, Certified Nurse Midwife – Birth Aesthetics Midwifery, USA

"Madison's depiction of rising from the ashes is honest and pure. You can't help but root for her in her quest for personal and professional excellence."

~ Chris Oeding, A two-time men's water polo Olympian and 2021 assistant coach of the USA women's Olympic water polo team, USA

"Madison's testimony is one of inspiration, empowerment, strength, and humility. She demonstrates the importance of being goal-oriented, driven to succeed, and finding one's passion in life."

~ Jennifer Mensching, Doctor of Occupational Therapy, USA

Reviews for Michelle Mehta

"The book inspires me to continue to share my message and really support our current and future generations to own their leadership. "

~ Mona Shaikh, Comedian and Producer, USA

"The book is very inspirational and motivates me to improve aspects of my life so I can put my best foot forward and live a healthier life."

~ Sahi Kollu, Corporate Finance, USA

"This book inspires women to be leaders and chase their dreams."

~ Sejal Shah, Energy Healer and Coach, USA

Book Reviews

Reviews for Monica Ward

"Monica shows us through the wonderful storytelling of her own 'heroine's journey' that visualizing the life we intend to lead in great detail can hold tremendous power!"
~ Michelle Harrington, owner of Outshine Fitness and Health Coaching, USA

"This just became one of those great books that I'll travel with, keep beside my bed, and gift to my team as we build. Everyone needs to learn and be reminded daily about the power of their thoughts and what they are actually capable of doing with them."
~ Jordan Sikes, Regional Brand Influencer-RevitalUSA

Reviews for Nurfadhlina Mohd Sharef

"Wonderful contributions, an eye-opener on the practicalities of data science and how it can impact others positively."
~ Associate Professor Dr Ts Mas Rina Mustaffa, Head of Department and Writer, Malaysia

"A story of how one woman pushes herself to fight the COVID-19 pandemic from spreading further in her country, Malaysia by making sense of the non-sense (data science). A raw and true story."
~Noris Mohd Norowi, Ph.D., Senior Lecturer in Computer Science and co-author of Srikandi PhD: Cerita, Cita-cita dan Cabaran (PhD Female Warriors: Stories, Ambitions and Challenges), Malaysia.

"The writer gave a great insight on data science. We never really appreciate the importance of it. She made it clear by explaining it in layman terms."
~ Ms. Ammielyya Jusnieza Ahmad Jafri, Science Communicator and Analyst, Malaysia

Reviews for Raeeka Yaghmai

"Raeeka's Love Education is truly a revolutionary concept, filling the void of correct information in this area of our life which every strong, educated, and successful woman must have. I highly recommend Raeeka's Love Education Academy to any woman who wants to feel as powerful and fulfilled in their love life as they do in their careers."
~ Dr. Nora Landburg, Psychotherapist, MFT

"When I read this, I felt Raeeka was describing my challenges with my love life. As a high-achieving woman, working in the "man's man" corporate world, I've often relied on my ivy league academic education to create my love life. I clearly see why I haven't been successful in this area. I'm excited to be a part of her Love Education Program. I feel like I finally have the right mentorship to create success in my love life."

~ Diana. B., Managing Director at Sutter Health

Reviews for Sara Ruda

"This is beautifully written. This lone, small piece of literature gave me strength to tackle the demons of self-hate due to the everyday things we deal with. I am my own worst enemy. I take a small criticism and turn it into a mountain of negative energy. Sara M. Ruda has dissected that feeling, that emotion that comes with trying to "be a leader, be a woman of power" and broken it into the pieces that you must understand to actually move forward. Again, beautifully written!"

~ Kendra Hausman, USA

"Sara M. Ruda is a hardworking and dedicated woman. She does not let anything bring her down, and if she does, she does not let it show. Her writing is very inspiring and reading about what she has experienced and accomplished is amazing."

~ Victoria Moseley, EMT, USA

"This chapter was amazing! It spoke to me in so many ways! It actually makes me think of myself and how she is talking to me! Learning to focus on my goals and not change them to make others happy has been one of my struggles. Reading this has reminded me of many situations where I need to work on myself. I look forward to reading and learning more from Sara M. Ruda!"

~ Sarah Heins-Satterfield, USA

Table of Contents

Foreword

The Key Ingredients That Create Formidable Female Founders

Bianca Barratt - a Senior Contributor to *Forbes Women*
- shares her insights on the traits the most impressive
female founders have in common.

As a Senior Contributor to *Forbes Women*, I've had the privilege to interview female founders from myriad backgrounds with a variety of expertise and am often asked if I can tell who will go far. Though I don't profess to hold a crystal ball, and no journey to success is the same, I have found that there are certain traits that distinguish those who thrive from those who don't.

Rather than having a good "business head," being excellent with finances, or having a knack for how to broker a deal or leverage investments – things that can be learnt by many – what sets the successful, the inspirational, the formidable apart from the rest is a handful of qualities. A handful of "ingredients," if you will.

Here's what I believe them to be:

Empathy

Empathy has, for a long time, been negatively viewed as a quality only held by the weak, but being able to put yourself in the shoes of someone else is vital in business. It allows you to connect with your employees and customers and visualise situations from another point of view. It's one of the highest forms of emotional intelligence.

A commitment to growth

The most inspiring female founders are humble enough to realise that they don't know everything and that, regardless of how much expertise or years of experience they have, there is still always an opportunity to learn. These founders go far because they do not rest on their laurels. They keep working and keep taking risks, so are continually developing their self-awareness which, in turn, makes them a better leader.

The ability to delegate

The greatest founders I've met have all been great at delegating – passing along opportunities and tasks to others in their team who can either learn from the experience or actually do a better job. This shows a generosity of spirit and commitment to true leadership that not many possess. It shows that they trust others to help them and allows them more space and time to work *on* the business rather than *in* it – something that's necessary to help it grow.

Integrity

Honesty sits at the heart of every successful founder's style. Without it, there is no trust – with employees or customers – and without trust, there is no business. Communicating honestly helps founders overcome challenges, makes it easy for people to connect with them, and helps them become more trustworthy. After all, people buy into people, and a founder who can be honest, even when times are hard, is truly inspiring.

Perseverance

Most female founders can recall at least one story of a door being closed on them, of being told "no," or that their idea wasn't good enough. The key trait that all successful female founders have in common is that they went through these challenges and didn't give up. The road up the mountain is long, but no matter how tough the journey, it's only those who keep going that get to enjoy the view from the top.

To those reading *Women Who Lead*, its contributors have showcased this spirit in their own lives and work. Read their chapters and embrace the lessons that resonate with you.

Good luck,

Foreword

Bianca

Bianca Barratt is a freelance lifestyle, culture, and business journalist and has written for titles including The Sunday Times, Refinery29, London Evening Standard, BBC Good Food, Independent, and Euronews. She is a Senior Contributor to Forbes Women and offers 1:1 consultations to founders looking to get themselves into the media.

Website: https://www.biancabarratt.com

From the book curator, Dr. Izdihar Jamil

Bianca is offering a 1:1 media strategy session for serious female entrepreneurs who want to be featured on high-profile publications such as *Forbes, Entrepreneur, Oprah,* etc.

Email: hello@izdiharjamil.com for more details on how you can have a 1:1 strategy session with **Bianca**.

Introduction

When I was curating this book, I had a vision of the women who were going to share their wisdom in this project. They are not the typical, "normal" women. They are the true trailblazers, the leader of the leaders in their respected fields. To get to where they are, they had to go through countless challenges, constantly up-leveling themselves, even though it's scary. No matter what happens in their lives, they are still standing tall and saying, "Here I am!"

Why?

Because when you are a true leader, you operate from a place where things are beyond you. You have a vision of how the world could look like. You remember the women who said to you, "You saved my life!" or "You made my dreams come true!" or when you see your little child smiling proudly at you for the things that you made happen after they see you crying. Those things that caused you to be unstoppable in are manifesting your vision.

The women in this book are beautiful, strong, smart, and absolutely extraordinary in being leaders in various areas of their lives. They share their hearts and wisdom to help you push through any adversity in your life because they know within you is a magnificent QUEEN!

These are real women with real results.

Darlings, if you're reading this book I know that you're someone special. I know you see something so big that sometimes it scares you. The principles and secrets that are taught in this book are your guide in manifesting the best version of your life. You only have one life, so you deserve to be the QUEEN in your QUEENDOM.

Many times I had to push through my own insecurities to get where I am today. What kept me moving forward was honing in the mantra that "I am the PRIZE."

You're UNSTOPPABLE, and may this book be the spark to light up your fire.

Here's to you leading your life with courage, love, integrity, and freedom while causing incredible results in your life.

You've got this, and so it is done!

Dr Izdihar Jamil, Ph.D.
Media Expert

PS: Want to be a Bestselling Author? I'd love to hear from you! Email me at: hello@izdiharjamil.com.

Women Who Lead

Julienne Waters

*"And the day came when the risk it took to remain tight inside
the bud was more painful than the risk it took to blossom."*
~ Anais Nin

Thoughts of a Working Mother

Many days I have cried.
I have been tested, I have been tried.
I have been buffeted by the storm.
I have been cold seeking the warm.
I have known pressure that felt like pain,
Yet I rallied again and again,
Not hugging to me the sting or the smart,
But trusting in goodness with all of my heart.
For its power upholds and never denies,
The pot of gold to the soul that tries.
I have lifted my spirit in prayer,
Wondering if God was really there;
I have felt lost, and sometimes alone,
But I took up my cause and moved on my own.
And as I went forward, I understood,
God is really the power of good.
Anytime I needed a friend,
I'd find that power waiting within.
I followed the only path I could take,
Sometimes so lonely my heart would ache.
My children but guessed, how could they know?
Leaving them daily would grieve me so.
It's rough going, but I do the best I could.
To plant in them the knowing, "Children, Life is Good!"

© **Pat Sampson**

Leadership Resilience

Julienne Waters
Transformation Stylist, USA

*"And the day came when the risk it took to remain tight inside
the bud was more painful than the risk it took to blossom."*
~ Anais Nin

Powerlessness

How could I ever have been so duped? Everything I thought was true, I now know was a sham!

My dad controlled us by abuse – he was abusive from day one of my life. Stories I've been told that even when I was in the womb, he threatened my mom at knifepoint, violently punching her in the belly.

But then, my parents found religion, and things got better. My dad stopped smoking, drinking, and discarded his knife collection. My chances at a normal childhood seemed bright, but it turned out the religion was a cult, and things became worse. I was subjected to every kind of abuse – physical, even more pervasive was the psychological, emotional, and spiritual abuse. One thing was always present – powerlessness.

One of the worst parts was having to be an "example," because as my dad was thrust into the spotlight, so was his family. We acted like outstanding members of the cult, even dressing "the part" as representatives of the church. First, my dad, now the church, does whatever it takes to CONTROL who I am supposed to be.

Later, as a married woman with five children, I was taking my children on the same path that I was forced to go down. Wasn't that what I was supposed to do? I was lost in my powerlessness.

Ground Zero

As I became more aware, I saw how deep the sexual abuse was in the cult.

1

This happened to both boys and girls from deep inside to the outside of the cult. Then it was my daughter, MY daughter, who was abused – and I had brought her there. I had brought all my children there. I felt devastated, enraged, and completely without support. I understood that this was not my fault, but it was my responsibility to take back control.

With my husband's support I, along with our five children ages four to 15, walked out of the cult and didn't look back. I summoned up all of my courage, gathered my children together, and began a new life. I knew I wanted to live in my personal power and help them to live in their power.

But at that time, I didn't know how to be a person, much less a parent. I was 36 years old, and my examples and teachers had not been good examples. They were horrible examples! The environment I grew up in never allowed me to be an individual. I didn't know myself. How was I supposed to know my children? How could I possibly be a good model for my children?

Growing up, I never fit in, never knew who I was. On the outside, I tried to look and feel the part of a good church member, and with my heart and mind shut down, I was always striving to conform. I learned to judge my internal feelings, thoughts, and actions. I walked on pins and needles all the time because I felt at any time, the rug could have been pulled out from under my feet if I were to deviate from the behavior that was accepted by the church. When I was with outside peers, the embarrassment, shame, and humiliation I felt was pervasive. I was unaware of it at that time, but somewhere inside me was exactly what I needed at the right time to break through this damaging upbringing.

I knew I had to start with myself from ground zero. The faint voice inside me grew louder and clearer, guiding me. By following this guidance, I gradually made myself over, becoming a new woman. The perfect teachers and coaches appeared, and I followed them. The migraines and depression I had suffered were lifted.

Without a Roadmap

Every decision I had made up until now from the perspective of the cult needed to be recalibrated. I was a victim and was holding on to that position, blaming, angry, and armored against the world. I unleashed myself on a journey without a roadmap, and into a world I had been taught to see as dangerous. All the perceptions that held me captive I now began to question.

Soon after leaving the cult, I divorced my husband, made radical changes, and faced new challenges as a single mom. And life doesn't stop, with five children. The demands of parenting, managing day to day, moment to moment all the responsibilities of school, cleaning, groceries, and laundry were never-

2

ending. I had to take time out for myself to grow and to have fun, have adventures and learn new ways of being. I took as many personal development trainings as I could.

It was with my teachers, Gay and Kathrine Hendricks, when I experienced a profound shift that I will be forever grateful for. I was taken aside on the last day of a workshop, and Katie asked me not to come back. I was showing up resistant and holding onto my victimhood. Tears began flowing down my face. I was devastated. Wasn't I the one who brought my friends to their training? Wasn't I the one who wanted so desperately to change?

Completely unaware that I was a victim and resisting the coaching, I immensely wanted to be there! Katie suggested that I do some serious introspection. When I was able to take responsibility, write her a letter, and she would consider my ongoing training. I had a choice to cower down or courage up. So, I chose courage, and a miracle happened. I softened inside and let go, and I became coachable. I began to learn from my story, not spiral over and over, forever getting lost in it.

The most predominate times were when my daughter unexpectedly died at age 23, and soon after remarrying my former husband 22 years after divorcing him, he was overtaken with cancer and passed away.

Gifts

Early in my life, I was blessed with gifts that I didn't appreciate. I lived in survival mode just about *all* the time. Now, I am grateful I lived through each of these experiences and have there gifts to draw from. As a child, I was naturally curious, adventurous, and imaginative. I hid through reading books to escape the abuse, which I devoured and discovered worlds that I could only imagine.

My parents, siblings, and I often moved – 29 times in 19 years, more than half of those in the same town. The resilience needed in this flux of constant change instilled in me is a great gift that I rely on to this day.

I grew up in Moab Utah, at the time, it wasn't the international destination that it is now, but a small town of 3,000. My parents, distracted with their commitments in the church, allowed us, my five siblings and me, to hike the red rocks. My father, a geologist, taught us "survival skills." Mom was overwhelmed, and to "get us out of the house," let us wander those rich red hills. So, at an early age, I developed a deep connection with the environment around me. I loved discovering plants and hidden creatures, vistas, and the sky with its ever-changing skyscapes. I pondered how life and existence were so incredible and so vast. I could feel the energy of the ancient wisdom around

3

me in the rocks, petroglyphs, and dinosaur footprints. I was constantly expanding my imagination and reverence for nature along with the Spirit of life. This was my nourishment and true spirituality.

Thank goodness for my love of knowledge, for my early beginnings, and my burying myself in books as an escape. Because as I read and grew, this became a blessing early on in my journey, and I came across this passage.

> *"This livingness that we're all in and of has*
> *something that reaches for freedom, a*
> *quality that may be a thread, and with an*
> *outstretched hand, it's there for you when*
> *you reach out for it; it will grab back."*
> ~ *The Fifth Sacred Thing,* by Starhawk

I now always feel this Spirit of livingness, as a divine presence. When I lose my way, I come back to this. I followed the Divine within. I had to learn to listen to this messenger, to accept, and invite a life more dynamic than I ever knew existed and then step into it.

The Blossom

What I know now is that life is a miracle. It can be an exquisite experience. It always gives you opportunities to grow.

I am in the business of transformation. This is how it happened…

Years ago, I felt I was in a default mode when I became a cosmetologist. You see, in the cult, I could have a trade, but not a "worldly" education! I had been cutting hair since I was 16 for my family and other cult members. But as a licensed stylist, I became independent and went into business. Little did I know I would become a successful entrepreneur. I developed my talent as a makeup artist, working with photographers. As an award-winning stylist, I had the honor of working with mayors, television stars, best-selling authors, and news anchors. Some of the trade lines I represented were Sebastian, Vidal Sassoon, Este Lauder, Aveda, Clinique, and many more.

It brings me great joy to see women glow when they love their reflection. The saying beauty is only skin deep is so not true! The beauty lies within. It needs to be encouraged and brought forward for the true radiance to shine. I have a gift of seeing the beauty within my clients,

I was making great money, I had an Aveda Lifestyle Salon and Spa, and yet the beauty industry was no longer fulfilling me. As I listened to clients'

4

struggles, I saw something missing in my clients, and that same thing was missing inside me. The missing piece was personal sovereignty and connection with the Divine. One can have a perfect look, but without tapping into the divine Spirit of greatness, it is only "Skin Deep!" I knew there was more for me to discover to grow myself and help my clients bring the true depth of their beauty to the surface. And I did just that... I amassed a body of transformational degrees and certificates and traveled the world working with thought leaders in the field of psychology and social change.

And then an unbearable thing happened. My daughter died. I was lost inside, desperately needing something to bring me back. Could I ever feel joy or be really alive again? I had to delve deeper.

The path inside this time came from an unexpected source. I met entheogens, plant medicines, and spirit teachers form one form, Ayahuasca. Again, my extreme discomfort brought me my courage. I took the leap, or shall I say, I took the elixir. When I did, a divine source cradled me with love and gave me an understanding of the universal dimension I had never known. Life and death made sense. I was healed of my extreme grief in the arms of this expansive, beautiful, loving Spirit. This love brought a new vision to me. Life opened up to new dimensions and possibilities.

In 2012, I began an in-depth immersion into the study of entheogenic medicines, becoming a member of the Multidisciplinary Association of Psychedelic Sciences. I was blessed to have studied with notable doctors, shamans, and healers, using psychedelics to heal emotional and spiritual trauma.

Conscious Leaders Are...

Through my journey, I've learned much about leadership. As an entrepreneur, as a woman, with tenacity, and resilience, I've become a leader.

1. Leaders are courageous and take radical responsibility.
2. Leaders are curious, always reflecting and learning.
3. Leaders are not stuck in their story; instead, they choose to vision big.
4. Leaders are positive thinkers.
5. Leaders are aware of their gifts and share them with the world around them.
6. Leaders are coachable.
7. Leaders are choosing to live their life as a leader.
8. Leaders are living in alignment with their highest self.

My Greatest Reward

I help motivated, professional women at the crossroads of their life create a path to live an extraordinary, courageous, and confident life by designing their lifestyle and personal style to align with their Divine higher self. The outside begins to reflect the inside, which radiates into the world as confident and impactful. When your light shines bright, it shows a way for others to follow and find their greatness. That is true leadership.

You have everything you will ever need within you. This Spirit of Life within you will never let you down, nor will it ever abandon you. You will begin to see that you are your life's creator and have the power. While you may not have control of some of the events in your life, you do have the option of HOW you think and grow as a result.

Perhaps like me, you have had an endless amount of suffering and hard lessons to learn. You may be stuck in your story and cannot escape. Perhaps you feel dull, resigned, or on automatic. Choosing to live a life of suffering will be a slow and painful road leading to depression, health disorders, anger, or overindulgence. Before you know it, this beautiful opportunity of life has slipped by. You may wake up one day, look in the mirror and ask the question, *Who is that woman?*, no longer knowing who you are or what you want. If you are uncomfortable enough, you know without a doubt that you are ready to reinvent who you are. So, choose to begin now!

Get in alignment with your purpose, knowing everything you need to have a fulfilled life is there for you. The Universe is waiting. As we reframe our thinking in alignment with our purpose, get curious, have gratitude, create a powerful vision, we become the curator of our life. When the world sees you transform, they want your aliveness. You become a model, or you choose to boldly step into your own brand, work your butt off, and launch your business. Either way, you are a leader. You model transformation!

How much better could it get?

Power Summary

1. There is a divine plan that is waiting for you to see. When you imagine it, consciously envision it, you can have the assurance that your higher self is waiting to fulfill your desires and live into your purpose.
2. So, create a miraculous, exquisite vision of yourself and your life. Make it glorious, spectacular, splendid, A life worth stepping into! Have courage, get curious, believe that you can have it! Whatever you want!

6

3. Anything you can envision, you can manifest. Thoughts are powerful. Retrain your brain and body to think in alignment with your vision. Make it your word; words are powerful. Speak it into being. In this way, you will bloom into your divine self.

Your most beautiful, amazing self is waiting for you to call.

Success Actions

1. Follow to my Divinely Envisioned Life Meditation Experience every day.
2. Journal about your meditation experience.
3. Daily, follow my Dynamic Breath Practice.

"When your discomfort meets your courage,
your power is at its peak! Grab it and create
an unstoppable You!"
~ Julienne Waters

For a Divine You,

Julienne Waters

About the Author

Julienne Waters is a life-transformation stylist who sees the hidden potential in her clients. She has been helping thousands of women for over four decades go from being unhappy with their lives to feeling confident and alive. She helps them envision their life as they want it to be in their highest state and brings out their courage to live it.

As someone who has overcome multiple traumatic events, Julienne is living proof of the magic of personal and image reinvention.

Julienne's travels have taken her to have many life-altering experiences. She has rafted white water on the Colorado River to the Pacuare River in Costa Rica. She made chocolate from a "bush to bar" with a remote indigenous tribe and even bungee-jumped in Bali. Julienne has marched with the famous Olodum percussion band in Salvador's Bahia, Brazil. She's ridden elephants in India and floated in a five-foot round basket on the Tungabhadra River while visiting the 10 temples in the surrounding area. She has danced the night away in the underground soirées in Paris and witnessed the powerful Spanish flamenco dancers up close in Madrid's century-old streets. She's wandered through many museums of art, studying modern artists and the greatest artists of 3,000 years ago.

In addition to her Earthly travels, Julienne has navigated the ethereal highways of the greater Universe, always seeking alignment with the Divine.

Contacts

Website: www.Divinelyblossom.com

Email: julienne@divinelyblossom.com

Social Media

Facebook: https://www.facebook.com/julienne.waters.1

TikTok: https://www.tiktok.com/@julienne_waters

Instagram: https://www.instagram.com/julienne.waters.1/

Free Gifts

Get my 10-minute guided meditation, and my 5-minute guided Dynamic Breath Practice by requesting it by email at divinelyblossom@gmail.com, and put in the Subject Line "Meditation Experience."

Make a Decision

Dr. Izdihar Jamil, Ph.D.
Media Expert, USA

"You're the PRIZE, every day, all day!"
~Dr. Izdihar Jamil, Ph.D.

The Birth

"Izzy, when do you think that the baby is coming out? In three to four hours maybe?" my midwife asked when I was in labor with my third child.

"God no, he's coming out in an hour!" I replied.

I opted to have a natural water birth, one of my dreams since my first child. There were no epidural or drugs to numb me. It was raw and extremely painful, but I trusted that my body could handle it.

So, when the midwife asked me if the baby was going to come in three to four hours, I made a decision that he was coming out within the hour. Darlings, there's no way that I was going to endure three to four hours of raw and unfiltered pain. Why subject myself to prolonged pain when I could end it as fast as I can and enjoy my bundle of joy?

And so, baby munchkin did arrive in less than an hour after I made the decision, and with God's help, I safely delivered a 6 lb 12 oz perfect little boy!

My midwife then said, "Izzy, you called it, less than an hour!"

Maddy, my Doula, who was my rock and supported me throughout my natural birth, said, "Izzy, that was a really powerful birth!"

From a decision that I made in my heart comes the verbal declaration coupled with the faith in God, and so… It Is Done!

The Circuit Breaker

Having a baby munchkin in my life is truly a miracle and blessing. I didn't think it would happen as I'm not in my 20s anymore, but God had other plans for me. He's adorable, cute, and full of joy. But he's also a complete circuit breaker in my life. My life isn't the same as before. His birth changes and interrupts many things in my life – my sleep, travel, schedule, relationships, and business. Everything changed within a blink of an eye.

Although since he's my third child, you would think that I've got it handled by now, right? Having two other kids before would mean that I've had some practice handling a baby. Yes and no. Yes, I remembered how to change the nappy, the nursing, and get through all the sleepless nights. But at the same time, I'm also older (okay, darlings, let's not calculate my age here!), have two other kids, and have a successful business of helping women become the number one go-to expert in their fields. With the two other kids, I didn't have a business. I left my secured job as a computer scientist to be a stay-at-home mom, support my husband and created the space so that my children would have the best life in America.

Running a business with two kids and taking care of my family – cooking, cleaning, doing the school run, helping my kids with their homework, and spending time with my husband – is a tough juggling act. Now, add all that with a baby that is totally dependent on you, and that's a completely new world altogether!

I was scared, worried, and anxious. Am I going to lose my ability to make money and my financial independence? How am I going to make it work with a baby and running a business? As cute as he is, he's unpredictable – there are no on-and-off buttons. He cries whenever he wants, sleeps whenever he feels like it, and does the number two whenever he chooses.

Yes, I could send him to daycare or hire a nanny, but in my heart, it's not something that I wanted to do. I want to hang out with him and enjoy my time with him. That's the whole reason why I created an online business so that I could have the freedom to work around my family. If you're a mom, you know that time flies so fast with our kids, and before you know it, they're an adult and don't want to hang out with you anymore.

What am I going to do? How can I have both my family and my business? How can I make it easier for myself? I was starting to panic and worry.

The Teacher

As I was contemplating my next step on how to figure out the solutions myself, one of my previous coaches, Carly Hope, who's a high-ticket sales mastery expert, reached out to congratulate me about my baby and asked how I was doing. She then mentioned that if I needed any help that she was here to support me because being a mom three times over is a game-changer.

You know the saying, darlings, "When the student is ready, the teacher will appear!" And that's exactly what happened to me because when I was in limbo on what to do, the best person meant to support me appeared. So I made a decision to ask Carly for support to figure out my next step to help me grow my business.

Tony Robbins said in his book *Awaken the Giant Within* that one of the keys to success is to make a decision. If you don't make a decision, a decision will be made for you. So, you can see, darlings, that to manifest your dreams, you have to start by making a decision. I made a decision for my baby to come within the hour. I made a decision to work with Carly to help support me while I'm in my transition and transformation phase.

With the decision set, I can now take the steps that align with my decision. I'm in control of what happens in my life because I've made a decision, set a goal, aligned myself with the best people to support me, and taken the necessary actions.

It's a Scary World

One of the scariest things about making a decision is whether I'm making the right decision or not. What if I made the wrong decision? Then things are going to be a mess. For example, I was scared to take on the coaching with Carly to help grow my business. What if I didn't have the money to pay her? Can I even do the work that she suggested? If I can't do the work, then I'll lose the money. Am I going to get the results I want? The reality was I'm in my nursing cocoon, so making money wasn't my priority then – baby munchkin was.

Brian Tracy, a leading success and human potential growth expert, said that we make mistakes 70% of the time. Well, how comforting is that, right? But then I've discovered that influential leaders are successful because of the mistakes they made. Why? Because that's how they learn, grow, and adapt. It isn't about making mistakes and failing. It's about growing, tweaking, and adapting as you go along that will separate you from the others who choose to play safe.

Every master was once a disaster. So it's okay to be messy. It's okay to mess up. The main thing is that I keep moving forward one step at a time. But the "ping-pong" session kept going on to the point that it was exhausting and draining me. I really wanted to move past this and get a clear yes or no to help me move forward.

The Decision-Making Rituals

Some of the things that I do to help me make a decision are the following rituals:

#1- Prayers. I would pray, put my head on the ground and ask God to guide me in making the best decisions for myself, my family, and my life. I feel that as human beings, our knowledge is just a dot compared to an infinite amount of knowledge and wisdom. And for me to tap into that unknown, that can only be accessed by seeking the help of the Creator.

#2- Open. I configured my heart, eyes, and senses to be open to any sign that God or the Universe are going to show me. Sometimes the signs are there, but I was too "blind" to see them. By being open, it helped me to see things that are meant to guide me in the right direction.

#3- Talking. I would share my ideas or reservations with the people in my trusted circle, like my husband and my best friend. Doing that is not to gain their validation, but just an opportunity for me to explore what's possible and at times listen to their insights informing me of things I may have missed. It's important that you share with the people that you trust that you know would support your dreams no matter how crazy they are instead of putting you down. You want to protect yourself from people who are going to put you down, poison your vision, or take away your light.

#4- Heart. I would close my eyes, take a few deep breaths, and just listen to my heart. The brain is the biggest trickster, but the heart never lies. I feel like the heart is our connection to the Divine Guidance. When it beats in a particular direction, I will listen to that beating and trust that it's the decision that's going to lead me to goodness and success.

#5- Question. I would ask myself, *"Is this decision going to help me get to my goals faster, or is it going to take me away from my goals?"* That would give me an indication as to whether I'm making the best decision or not.

Once I've got clarity and the guidance that I needed, I make the decision and take actions consistent with the decision. Actions lead to results. In my case, I made a decision to go with Carly, and I've never looked back. It turns out I was rapidly able to grow my business while enjoying my time with baby munchkin, but it took a transformation on my business structure to be able to play at that high-energy level.

My Biggest Wisdom

Since making the decision that, *"Yes, I need help, and I'm going to choose to work with Carly!"* or *"Baby munchkin is coming within the hour!"*, I've implemented several new structures to my business based on our discussion.

It truly does have an impact when you work with someone who's a few steps ahead of you because they can hash things out and see things that you couldn't see.

If you've read this far, darling, I know that you're someone special. I know that you're committed and serious to have the best life and be the best version of you that you can be. I know that you have the ability within you to be the true leader that you are. You just need to figure out how to unlock and unleash your power to help you to move forward.

Knowing what I now know, here are my top five tips for you to help you grow your business and career:

#1 – Goal

Set yourself a crazy goal that you've never done before. I know you might be thinking, *"I don't want to create a crazy goal because when I don't hit it, then it means that I'm a failure!"* Here's a secret, darling, when you set a goal, you don't set it from your current self; you set your goals from your future self. Your current self is the beta or the trial version of you, but your future self is the bigger, more powerful version of you.

For example, your current self would set a goal like, *"I will make $10,000 a month consistently,"* because it is a safe and doable goal. But your future self would set a goal like, *"I will make $100,000 or more a month consistently."*

Will you fail in setting for yourself that outrageous goal? Maybe, and maybe not, but it would push you to be who you've never been before. It would pull you to take massive, courageous actions. I mean, wouldn't you rather take $50,000 a month than $10,000 and be happy with it? If so, then you'll start to tweak things to make it better, and pretty soon, making $100,000 or more a month will be your new normal.

Remember, there is no such thing as a bad goal, only an unachievable timeline. So, all you have to do is adjust your timeline and tweak your actions. Doing that will bring you faster to your goals.

#2 – Team

One of my biggest limitations with a baby is that I can't go on as many sales calls as I did before. I'm often up multiple times at night nursing, and I'm tired by the afternoon. Also, with a baby, taking care of him is my priority. Though it sounds empowering to bring my baby on calls with me, the truth is I'll be lucky if he lasts 15 minutes on the call without needing my attention. It's also exhausting for me to be on calls while nursing or looking after a baby. It means that I have to work double or triple harder all the time.

So, I created a team of fabulous women to support me. For example, I enrolled three incredible ladies who happened to be my previous clients to help me with the sales calls and administration work.

In the beginning, I was like, *"Why would anyone want to be part of my team?"* and, *"Who can I trust with my business?"* But Carly said that the best person is usually right in front of me, and she's someone who believes in me and my services. I was also scared to invite people into the intimate part of my business. I was afraid that I would get hurt or wondering if I could trust them.

Then I asked God to show me to the best person that is trustworthy, kind-hearted, and committed to helping grow my business, and in return, I would be able to help them too. I'm thankful that I've been guided to work with three amazing ladies, and together, we become the unstoppable "Team Diamond Queens!" "Diamond" because the more challenges that we face, the shinier and more expensive we become. In a few years, I could see our Team Diamond growing and be unstoppable because our heart and mission are aligned.

#3 – Retreat

My previous method of leveraging myself on a 1:1 basis didn't work anymore. If I wanted to reach thousands of women fast, I had to figure out a way to leverage myself. Rather than giving people me, I would give them a system.

Since my work is about helping female entrepreneurs and coaches to be the #1 go-to expert in their fields, I created a FREE virtual retreat for women called "The Top Authority Activation Retreat." It's an exclusive and safe space for women to support each other. Inside the retreat, I would give high-value content to create the know-like-love trust factor with my tribe before inviting them to work with me.

I love nurturing women in an intimate space, and with just a video, I can help so many women at the same time. I know that the women in my tribe love to have an intimate, warm, and connecting space to learn and grow. Since the pandemic, instead of going to a physical retreat, I created a virtual retreat so the women in my tribe can hang out while I deliver high-value content. This not only helps to increase my trust and credibility factors with my audience, but it also made it easy for me to upsell my services because I've already nurtured a relationship with them.

You can join my "Top Authority Activation Retreat" at:

https://www.izdiharjamil.com/fast-authority.

I'd love to see you there!

#4 – Offers

To hit my goal of working only two to three hours a day and only making three sales calls a week, I had to create a new set of offers that not only will serve my women but help me to hit my income goal with ease and speed. I figured out what my women wanted and created several attractive packages for them.

I named each package based on precious metals because I know that's something that my women could relate to. My starter package is called "Silver," then comes "Gold," "Platinum," Sapphire," and finally "Diamond," which is my highest package.

My Diamond Package is for those special women who are so ready to be heard, seen, and be unleashed to thousands and millions of other women because they are called to a higher purpose of serving others. Imagine your business, message, and brand being seen on *Amazon* as a Bestselling Book, on TV, in magazines, hundreds of globally trusted media, and high-profile platforms such as *Forbes*, *TEDx*, and *Oprah*...

Would that help you to get the best clients and make the most money?

Would that help fill your heart with so much joy and contentment, knowing that you are serving your purpose by helping thousands of others?

I would say, "HECK YES!" to that. But it takes an extraordinary woman to be in my Diamond Package. Regardless, I have it prepared in advance for when the right women appear, and when they do, I am ready to go, and so are they.

I've crafted each package carefully, giving them irresistible and outrageous value that it's a no-brainer for them to say YES as long as they are ready to move forward. That's key, darling. Your potential clients have to be ready and committed so that both you and them are a good fit. Don't feel rejected if they say no. You've done your best at that time, so keep moving forward no matter what.

What is meant for you will never miss you, and what misses you was never meant for you. Trust in the abundance, let go of any attachments and just flow.

#5 – Exclusivity

Because what I'm offering are premium services, I created them for my team and me to be exclusive. That means that we are not available to everybody, but only to those selected few who meet our criteria. I absolutely love working with serious, committed women who are ready to take the step to become the go-to expert in their fields. In return, they love working with me because I have the best-proven system to help them get on various multi-media platforms.

I also created my package to be in a higher-end price range. Ken Honda said in his book, *Happy Money*, that it doesn't matter what price you put on a product; there will always be clients. It's just different kinds of people buying it. With a higher price range, I'm attracting high-quality, serious women who are committed to doing the work. They also appreciate the high-value services that I offer them.

I've stopped chasing people or becoming a "desperado." I set my standards and keep myself grounded. I imagine myself as a lighthouse that stands proud, tall, and strong regardless of the weather condition. And in that strength, I would continue to shine my brightest light so that people can be drawn to me because I'm their beacon of hope by being grounded and still. I know that my women will come to me because we both said YES to each other, which makes us the perfect fit.

In other words, I am the prize, and so are you, darling!

Power Summary

Okay, darlings, let's summarize the key points for you to take away from my chapter:

1. What is one decision-making ritual that I mentioned in my chapter?

2. What is one tip that I mentioned that can help you to grow your business or career?

3. Fill in the blanks. I am the _____.

Key Actions

Let's get you moving closer towards your goals by taking the following actions:

1. Set one outrageous goal. Write it down.

2. Create a new high-end offer that can help you to hit your goals faster. For example, a $10,000 or $20,000 package.

3. Make one decision today that can help you to move closer to your goals. For example, hiring a new team member.

> *"I've worked hard for a long time, and it's not about winning. What it's about is not giving up. If you have a dream, fight for it!"*
> ~ Lady Gaga, Oscar-Winning Speech, 2009

Make a Decision

All the best and remember, you're the PRIZE!

Izdihar

Dr. Izdihar Jamil, Ph.D.

About the Author

Dr. Izdihar Jamil, Ph.D., is an immigrant, Asian, hijab-wearing Muslim computer scientist turned media expert.

She is an eight-times #1 International Bestselling Author of *It Is Done*, *Yes I Can!*, and *Women Who Lead* and has spoken in hundreds of prestigious events and interviews all around the world. She was featured on *Forbes*, Fox TV, NBC, CBS, ABC, CW, *Thrive Global*, and hundreds of media and publications.

In 2021, Izdihar was inducted into the prestigious *Marquis Who's Who* biography along with Warren Buffet and Oprah, recognizing her contribution as being in the top 5% of the industry. She is also an upcoming *TEDx* presenter sharing her idea about Authenticity During Social Adversity to inspire marginalized women to be confident with their heritage and roots.

She is an influential trailblazer and an inspirational leader in helping female entrepreneurs be the #1 go-to expert in their fields with her simple, no-fuss methods. She has helped over 100 people be a #1 International Bestselling Author and get in online media, magazines, high-profile interviews, and publications.

Izdihar lives in California with her husband and three kids, and in her spare time, she loves reading and baking for her family.

Contacts

Website: www.izdiharjamil.com

Join my FREE Top Authority Activation Retreat for Women to help you be the #1 go-to expert in your field:

https://www.izdiharjamil.com/fast-authority

You can check out my Bestseller book, *It Is Done! 15 Secrets To Manifest Your Dream Life*, on Amazon.com.

Facebook: https://www.facebook.com/drizdiharjamilphd

LinkedIn: https://www.linkedin.com/in/drizdiharjamilphd/

Instagram: https://www.instagram.com/izdiharjamil/

Twitter: @IzdiharJamil

Center First! Then Act

Marcia Martin
Internationally Renowned Thought Leader, USA

"You either have the results you want in life,
or the reasons you don't have them."
~ Marcia Martin

The Meltdown

The email came through early in the morning, and as I read it my blood went cold. Everything I had planned and hoped for was crumbling as I read those horrible words: *"Termination of Agreement."*

Only days before, my team and I had been celebrating our good fortune of finally finding the Branding & Marketing Company and closing the deal that was set to be the foundation for us in building and launching my digital training products that would culminate in multi-million-dollar profits. All our years of work had paid off. We were finally set to take off! We had secured the guidance of experts in branding and marketing at a fee that we could accommodate; the branding expert that would be running the project was passionate about me and my work and products; and he was delighted to be involved with me and my team, he was committed to my vision, and he realized the extraordinary product possibilities of my gift of training others to achieve championship performance in business and in life.

As I read the email further, I feared all that I had put together for the future three-month launch was down the toilet. He could not commit after all. He had terminated our agreement and again I was left alone and isolated, not knowing my next move, nor how to take my new digital company forward.

A feeling of anxiousness welled up inside, and my mind shouted at me,

"This isn't fair! He promised! How could he do this?" My breath was going short, my head was pounding, and I wanted to scream. I immediately started typing, *"Please, please, can we meet and discuss this further?"* I hoped I could talk him into changing his mind. Fortunately, I did not actually send the email, but I did type up a storm, as I laid out a few insults and incriminations.

I had just the day before told my colleagues that it was happening. I had already set up meetings for the following week to start the process of getting pieces in place, and people collaborating and moving. *"No! No! No! Do I now have to call everything off?"*

I could see by the email that the refund to me was already in process. I felt like I was drowning. *"What should I do now? Who could I turn to?"* This had been the answer to everything we had needed, to everything I had worked for, to everything that had been uncertain before.

I ran to the shower and gave myself a good dose of cold water and started to cry. I felt so helpless. I didn't have time to start over with the process of finding another Branding & Marketing Company – I was leaving the following week to go abroad, starting on a tour of weeks of training I would be facilitating in 3 different countries. Everything I had put in place was now in jeopardy and I had no time to even salvage it before I left on my trip.

People were counting on me and on the profits that would come in to fund their lives and families as a result of the launch. I thought I had it all figured out, and here it now seemed as if it had all gone down the drain.

As I stood there in the shower, cold water pouring down on me, my mind screaming at me, a small voice began to emerge from the depths of my Soul, reminding me of a better course of action. *"Marcia, remember what you teach people. Remember to 'center' before you act. Bring yourself back to 'center'. Remember, you will always have one or the other – the result you want in life, or the reasons you don't have that result. Get yourself 'centered' and focus on the result you want, instead of all the circumstances that look like they may get in the way."*

I began to breathe more easily again, and to settle down from that horrible feeling of falling off a cliff with no parachute.

The Turning Point

I have learned that the Turning Point in Life is not when things miraculously turn around and life becomes a series of wins, when previously it might have been a series of losses. Instead, the Turning Point – for me – in life is when one starts to realize that life is a journey and process of both wins and losses – and the 'breakthrough' is not the result you have in the end, but rather the way you handle the circumstance you find yourself in, in the first place.

Center First! Then Act

The whole journey of Life is filled with wins and losses; one doesn't magically go from a life that doesn't work, to a life that works. That's silly. That's not the 'turning point'. The turning point is when you are consciously able to observe yourself in the breakdown moments and then turn yourself around to be able to create a breakthrough result. And there will be many opportunities for that along the path of life – because "That's Life!".

Life is not, in my interpretation, a *black and white matter* – a matter of breakdown **OR** breakthrough. One's life isn't 'Not Working', one day: and then suddenly 'Working Well' the next day. It is, and always will be, a process. Life is *'Shades of Grey'*.

My life is unique and unusual due to the training and mentoring I received as a young girl. By the time I was in my early 20's I had already studied all the world religions and great philosophers, I had already participated in thousands of personal development trainings and programs, I had already been mentored by some of the greatest academic thought leaders of our time including acclaimed futurist and visionary Buckminster Fuller, personal development guru Werner Erhard, Oscar-winning film-producer Jerry Weintraub, influential business scholar and consultant Peter Drucker, and renowned pioneer of leadership studies Warren Bennis.

As such, I was given the educational and philosophic tools needed to face life's breakdown situations in a way to accomplish breakthrough results at a very early age. So, I personally had *no **major** breakthrough* which changed my life or 'turned it around'. My life was on the path of success, joy, personal development, and growth from the moment I learned to meditate at age 12 when I first read *Atlas Shrugged* by Ayn Rand.

I had been taught, throughout my life, and as I teach other in my *Talk This Way Leadership & Communication Programs* ™, how to cause circumstances, rather than be at the effect of them; how to deal with my emotions when they came up; and how to be present and centered to create and implement productive and powerful choices, rather than deal with life in reaction to outside events.

The Impact and Lesson

After I got myself centered that morning, and I could breathe easily again, instead of gasping for air in panic, then I began to consider my options. Being in a state of upset, as I had previously been when not centered, that was impossible, but now getting myself back into 'present-time' and out of the panic-mode, I could consider choices I had, rather than operating from emotional reactions and fear.

I've personally trained over 300,000 around the globe, and that is the fundamental first step I teach people to do in all situations, and especially in panic-driven and upsetting circumstances: *Center First – Then Act.*

We experience life's events in one of two ways. Either:

- An event in life, or circumstance reminds us of an earlier traumatic experience we had previously in life, which 'triggers' the old event in our mind, and then we 'act-out' in automatic 'default' behaviors of the same sort we originally used during that old trauma that seemed to work then – as a REACTION.

    Or...

- We are aware consciously that the circumstance is 'triggering' us; and we first come back to 'center' (a popular topic in my *Talk This Way Trainings* ™) and get ourselves back in present-time where we are not caught up in the old default behavior pattern of the old trauma, and in that 'centered' place we are able to RESPOND with choice, rather than REACT, and actually choose consciously our next behavior, speech, and action which will influence and impact the current circumstance and produce positive and constructive movement forward.

It took me a bit of time, and some discipline to 'center' myself that morning. It was a back-and-forth-motion at first. First, I was centered, then I thought about the email, and I got upset again. Then I had to consciously discipline myself to breathe, to let go of all the raging thoughts in my head, and to pull myself back from the upset into present time. I even sat down in a chair, closed my eyes, and focused on my breath in meditation for a few moments, actively making my breaths deeper and longer, and slowing my heartbeat. Back and forth. Back and forth. Upset, calm, upset, calm.

But I did not write the final email until I was able to stay in that calm state for an extended period, to be able to create an email that was productive, rational, and something that could open a positive and constructive conversation.

Then, before I sent it, I imagined the worst scenario and the best scenario and allowed myself to be at peace with each one. Then I pushed the SEND button, asking for a meeting to discuss the situation further.

That day, I re-remembered the lesson and value of 'centering', that I have taught so many. Rather than feeling panicked and acting as if I was a victim, and then proceeding to come up with all sorts of blaming judgments about someone else, or incriminating opinions of myself I started seeing the possibility of new options and I felt a sense of freedom and peace. From that place, I was able to envision a much more compassionate, understanding, and creative conversation that could take place.

And because of that, when we talked, we were able to come up with more creative possibilities and ideas for us to work out a solution. Instead of me blaming him for backing out of an agreement or making him feel guilty about my personal and professional repercussions, I was able to compassionately listen to his explanation of what turned out to be, a situation out of his control. And together we worked out a new solution.

Again, I was also reminded of my mantra: *You either have the results you want in life, or the reasons you don't have them.* I could have spent time making up all sorts of reasons why this all didn't work out the way I wanted:

- He didn't give me all the information I needed in the first place.
- He didn't look at all the necessary aspects of the project.
- I didn't have time to work it out with someone else.
- I picked the wrong person to work with.
- You can't trust people after all.

But instead, I centered myself, and focused on how to make it work, rather than on all the reasons it wasn't working. I also chose to face the situation as if it was meant to be and as if the way life works is that if one door closes, then another one opens that is even better.

I trust in FLOW – if I am aligned with my personal inner power and higher Self, and if I stay centered and in present time, and if I stay focused on the results that need to be produced instead of getting caught up in all the breakdowns, obstacles, excuses, and upsets of the moment; then I trust that the best thing will happen to produce the best result. I operate as if the Universe may know better than me what that is, and I do my best to accept the Universe's gifts – which, as I see it, are the experiences I have in my Life, whatever they may be.

I considered that it was possible that the termination of the agreement might be a positive event rather than getting upset about it, reacting with blame, and considering it something that was horrible and wrong. I stopped resisting the way it was playing out, I stopped acting like a child having a temper tantrum about not getting what I thought I wanted and started focusing on how this could work instead.

And, like magic, it worked out even better than I had originally planned. I ended up creating a better agreement, and a better plan moving forward than had been there in the first place. And the branding expert found a way to guide me to that better path, so he felt better in the long run as well. A real win-win.

My Personal Story

I'm just like every other human being – I have pain, I have loss, I experience anger and fear, and sometimes – in fact, many times – life is a struggle. I don't have all the answers and things don't always work out the way I want them to.

I've been through a painful divorce after my husband cheated on me; I've lost millions of dollars when a business failed; I've been betrayed by a close colleague who spread lies about me, and my business reputation and credibility suffered as a result; I've lost a step-son to suicide, and two brothers to addiction and crime; I've been estranged from family members over family disagreements; and I've felt lonely and isolated being by myself without a mate for years.

When I was a young girl my aunt taught me about metaphysics, Universal Laws, and how to meditate and work with energy and healing arts. When I was a young woman, I was fortunate to be in the right place at the right time, and I was a Founding Member of a new entrepreneurial organization that became one of the largest personal development and education companies in the world – *est (Erhard Seminars Training)* which is now known across the globe as the *Landmark Forum.*

For 10 years from inception, I was the Executive Vice President and helped take the *est* organization from an original seminar of 20 participants to thousands of seminars and millions of graduates worldwide. I learned how to train others to find and awaken their inner personal power, and to be master communicators and leadership champions.

After I left *est (Landmark Forum)* in 1980, I partnered with one of the leading fashion jewelry designers of our time – Laurel Burch – and we created *Tsuru, Inc.*, a Fashion Jewelry Design & Manufacturing Company with offices in Hong Kong, New York, Los Angeles, and San Francisco, with over 3,500 wholesale clients including *Neiman Marcus, Bloomingdales,* and the *Smithsonian Museum*; we were awarded some of the very first USA contracts by the *People's Republic of China,* before China was opened to the rest of the world.

Having also consulted for many of the top transformational thought leaders of the *Personal Development Industry,* including Jack Canfield *(Chicken Soup for the Soul),* Tony Robbins *(Unlimited Power),* Bob Hoffman *(The Hoffman Process),* and John Hanley *(Lifespring),* I learned the rewards of service, and to contributing to making this a better world for all, which I continue to hold as an important personal commitment.

Since that time, and for the past 40 years, I have created and managed my own Executive Training Firm - *Marcia Martin Productions, LLC* - and I work with many powerful organizations, training their senior executives in leadership development and communication competency. My clients include *Hard Rock Hotels International, Warner Bros., Capital One, McCain Foods, Evian Water, InterContinental Hotels, Loews Hotels, Hyatt Hotels*, and *Dannon Yogurt.* I also lead *Talk This Way Workshops and Leadership Programs* ™ for the public domain, as well as for corporate clients. And I have a successful *Executive and Life Coaching Program.*

I'm just like everyone else in the world when it comes to struggle and heartache. But I've had the opportunity to have great mentors and teachers who showed me how to create a healthy mindset and how to access and harness my inner power. It's now my life's work to help others do the same: I design and facilitate training programs that help people transform their lives into powerful and effective human beings so they can accomplish all their dreams.

Key Lessons of Wisdom

Hopefully these thoughts I offer will reach into your heart and be of help when you are upset, or when things don't go well for you, when you have 'bad' days, or when things don't end up the way you'd ultimately planned.

Wisdom Lesson # 1 – Center First, Then Act

Lots of times we find ourselves off-center, upset, confused, rattled by events and circumstances, angry at others, or fearful of things. During these times, remember before you speak, before you take any action of any kind – remember to center yourself first. Get back to the present time. Get out of your head and out of your emotions. Take a deep breath. Calm yourself down. Allow whatever is happening to happen the way it is happening, rather than resisting it. After you have centered yourself, and only then, choose how you will respond. Otherwise, you will be reacting, not responding with purpose and choice, and your results will suffer.

Wisdom Lesson # 2 – Focus on the Results You Want, rather than the Reasons for not Having Results

It's easy to start making up reasons, justifications, and excuses for not having results that then become the focus of our conversation and observation. That will take us off course. Keep your focus on the *result* you intend, rather than letting your mind wander to the *excuses* that justify not having those results.

Wisdom Lesson # 3 – Confront in Your Mind What Might be the Possible Outcomes

If we can handle something in our Minds, we can handle it when it happens. Imagine the possible outcomes – the worst it could be, and the best it could be. Get to a place with yourself that is OK either way. It is just the way it possibly might be. Nothing more than that. That is a place of acceptance. That will allow you to focus on the intention you have, rather than having your focus on resisting what you don't want. Once you do that in your Mind, the chances are that the actual result will work out better, or at the very least you won't be upset with however it works out – rather, you will be able to deal with it rather than getting upset and swept away by your emotions.

Success Assignments

Here are some assignments you can do in your own life, that will begin to change the way you act, speak, listen to, and see others, which will increase your ability to produce better results and get better outcomes:

- Start to be aware of what 'triggers' you. Use your awareness to prepare yourself when you think those things may happen. Go into the situation with your eyes wide open.

- When you are 'triggered', instead of immediately reacting to the situation out of emotion or automatic default behaviors, first 'center' yourself, then choose consciously a response that can forward the situation in a productive manner. Intentionally choose a response rather than automatically reacting.

- When you notice you are 'off-center', focus on getting back to center. Be aware of what it takes, what works, what can bring you back to present time. Have your attention on getting back to center faster than you did the last time the same thing put you off-center. You will never be centered all the time because you have emotions, but practice getting back to center faster each time.

- Begin to focus on having the RESULT you intended; do not be satisfied with the excuses you make up for not having the result.

- When you want something badly, imagine both the worst and the best that could possibly be the outcome – until you can look at both with no emotion, but with a simple observation of *"Yes, that's possible, and it's ok."* That will allow you to better confront what does happen in a way that is positive rather than disabling.

For Continued Growth

Thousands of people around the world write to me and say I have changed their lives for the better. I'm thrilled when I hear comments like, *"You saved my marriage." "My sales and profits have doubled." "I am confident when I speak in public now and I love it." "I never dreamed life could be so good." "I don't get upset anymore about things that used to throw me into a rage."*

If you are interested in finding out more about me, or in participating in some of my Programs, then go to one of these Websites for more information:

https://www.marciamartinclub.com/

https://www.marciamartin.com/

*"Be willing to be uncomfortable in life.
There is no growth in the comfort zone."
"My life's work is having your life work
better."*
~ Marcia Martin

With love to all,

marcia martin

CEO
Marcia Martin Productions, LLC

About the Author

Dame Marcia Martin (knighted in 2012 for her humanitarian efforts) is known by colleagues as the Human Potential Movement's Godmother of Transformation. As CEO of Marcia Martin Productions, LLC, and innovator of the Talk This Way™ Leadership Development Programs, she is a renowned global speaker, executive trainer, and life coach who empowers individuals and corporate teams to transform their businesses, relationships, and lives. She has consulted various Fortune 1000 Corporations, including Hard Rock Hotels International, Warner Bros., McCain Foods, Dannon Yogurt, Evian Water, Capital One, and InterContinental Hotels, to achieve communication mastery, diverse cultural collaboration, and championship performance. She has personally trained over 300,000 individuals worldwide. Ms. Martin was the Senior Vice President and an original Founding Member of "est" (Erhard Seminars Training, now known as the Landmark Forum), the largest personal development educational company of our time. She was instrumental in taking the Company from inception to a graduate base of millions within ten years. She has been featured on CBS News, FOX, NBC, and ABC. Marcia's mission is to transform a person's Mindset to operate as champions, empowering them to access and harness their inner power to create a more conscious and effective World for all.

Contacts

Marcia Martin Productions, LLC

Phone: +1 818-395-5637

Email: Marcia@MarciaMartin.com

Websites: www.MarciaMartin.com
               www.MarciaMartinClub.com

Office: 6654 Villa Sonrisa Drive, Suite 420, Boca Raton, Florida 33433, USA

Faking It Till You Make It?

Amber Howard
Canada

"Love, connection, and belonging are
fundamental to our wellbeing and success."
~ Amber Howard

I will never forget the moment I was exposed! I was sitting in my co-worker's office meeting regarding a project when my director poked her head in the door. She was there to make a last-ditch plea to have me participate in a photo opportunity for an award that I helped my team win. I had gone to Boston to receive the award, and both my manager and director really wanted me to be a part of the photoshoot. I was a firm no!

Shannon wasn't there to pressure me, and I had an immediate emotional response to the request; tears welled up in my eyes. The thinly veiled mask I always wore had cracked, and I was both embarrassed and angry. I had been found out, and part of me was furious with my boss and friend for exposing me. You, see up until five years ago, I was a woman who walked through life carrying profound shame and self-loathing. You would never have known it to look at me. I walked through life head held high, never letting anyone see my biggest weakness – I hated myself!

I had made many "mistakes," getting pregnant at 16, dropping out of high school, "disappointing" my family and community, marrying an abusive man at 18 – my personal record of my shame seemed endless. To fix these errors in judgement, I became driven – driven to prove I was worthy, to prove I wasn't powerless to create a better life for my children. I left their father at the age of 20, and from inside, my private hell of shame and self-loathing sought to make it "right."

"Shame" is defined as the belief that there is something about us that, if seen or known by others, would make us unworthy of connection and belonging. For much of my life, I walked around surrounded by people but completely alone. I took care of everything and everyone else, put my needs last, tried to be a "good" person, all to redeem myself. You see, therein lies the problem of shame because you can't fix a problem created in your mind, in reality. No matter how hard I worked, or how successful I became, or how many good deeds I had done, none of it altered the view I had of myself inside my own mind. These destructive habits of self-loathing, martyrdom, and attempted atonement continued to be hidden from my view for most of my life. Until, that is, October 14th, 2016!

I was standing at the front of a room with 150 strangers. At the suggestion of a dear friend, I chose to participate in a personal development course. The leader was coaching me through a conversation about the things that happen in our lives and the stories we make up about them, and what we make those stories mean about us – how they become the truth.

When I was 17 years old, a few months after the birth of my eldest son Matthew, I was physically assaulted by the man I loved, the father of my son. I still recall the fear and deep shame I experienced when remembering him holding his hand at my throat. I knew there must be something wrong with me. I decided I was powerless and worthless. What followed were decades of creating and collecting evidence to prove myself right about the story I had created at that moment.

Standing at the front of that room, 20 years later, I discovered this story had been running my life, hidden from my view. In that room, I discovered the truth about myself that until that point in time I was unable to see. You see, I didn't have a small self-esteem problem. I was still so unworthy that the entire world could have told me that they loved me, and I would have made liars of them all.

I drove home from the course that night sobbing with remorse for the impact my story had on my children and those I loved. The Monday morning following my course, I woke up in a brand-new world. It was literally as if a line had been drawn in the sand. There was life before that weekend and life afterwards.

During the course, I discovered many tools that allowed me to overcome my self-esteem issues. One of the biggest was really understanding that beating up on ourselves and experiencing shame is just part of what it is to be a human being. Almost all of us deal with the seemingly unrelenting voice in our heads.

You see, herein lies the paradox of what it is to be a human being. We are hardwired for love, connection, and a desire to belong, and yet shame causes us to walk through life disconnected and alone, not able to be seen. Shame has us sell out on what we truly desire, which is to be accepted and belong. Fear of failure, of what others will say and think, has us not fully show up in life. We settle for what we know we can have. Many never even inquire into what they authentically want. This inquiry is, in fact, the starting point of creating a life we love, based on our own measures for success and happiness. This is a life where we are not looking outward to societies, our families, or peers' standards, and instead, defining for ourselves what living the life of our dreams would look like as our own unique expressions. To even begin this inquiry, we first have to realize we are worthy of having our hearts desires.

Discovering the answer to the question "What do I WANT?" was the starting point of a complete transformation of my life. Through many years of personal development, I continue to unpeel the layers of my relationship with myself. I discover ongoingly that love of self isn't a place to arrive at; it's an ongoing journey to self-discovery, of unpacking the limiting beliefs hidden in the subconscious mind. Beyond the many tangible results, such as building a six-figure business where I serve the best clients all over the world, living in an incredible home, having the most incredible relationships with my children, falling in love with the partner of my dreams (after 13 years of being single), the most extraordinary outcome of all is that my view of self is a match for how the world sees me.

I am a generous, fierce, and fun force of love. A woman whose leadership is a focal point for the transformation of humanity, an individual who will leave a legacy of love for the world. I have journeyed to the center of myself and discovered that miracles are possible when you embrace your entire self, everything that works and everything that doesn't, with no invalidation, only grace and total acceptance.

I've shared with you my personal journey from shame to falling head over heels in love with myself and the difference this has made in every area of my life. What this has made available is living the created life of my dreams. What's amazing about the life I get to lead today is it was so unpredictable! I was born in New Zealand to parents who both experienced extensive childhood trauma and were themselves born into generational cycles of pain and shame. I was raised by my mother, and after what was a somewhat nomadic and comparatively idyllic childhood, immigrated to Canada at the age of 10. Upon arriving in Canada, life quickly became traumatic and is most definitely the topic of another book. What I want you to know about my journey is that I have become highly resilient, profoundly grateful, with crystal clarity about who I am and my purpose on this planet. Inside this purpose, it is my privilege to be a leader of leaders. I am honoured to facilitate female leaders to fulfil their purposes. I get to wake up daily, and in partnership, create a world that works for us all. I wake up every day in love with myself and my life!

Key Lessons and Words of Wisdom

I LOVE learning! There are few things I enjoy more than personal discovery, learning, deepening my understanding of self and the world around me. I love to learn both for the difference my ongoing development has made in my life and because it allows me to be an even bigger contribution to others. These lessons and words of wisdom have made a massive difference in the results I achieve and my experience of life, as well as for my many students, clients, and those I coach – really anyone whose life I am blessed to touch. These strategies will elevate your life!

Wisdom #1 – Accountability Ensures Success

Accountability is your insurance against failure. Let's just talk straight – commitments and promises disappear! One minute we say we want something for our lives, whether it's to lose weight, earn more money or launch a new business, and the next, we are doing the opposite of what we know works. Have a coach, accountability partner, or group of people that will hold space for the things you say matter. Going it alone is not the answer, especially in those areas of life where we have felt stuck or resigned.

Wisdom #2 – Your Circle Matters

Surround yourself with people who speak life into you. It's been said that you are the sum of the five people you spend the most time with. Who are you spending time with? Are they engaged in activities that are aligned with the kind of life you want to live? Are your friends your biggest cheerleaders, or are they constantly arguing for what's not possible? Are the conversations you are having, the kinds of people you are giving and receiving energy with the kinds of people who will elevate your life, or are they dragging you down?

Wisdom #3 – Your Map of the World is Not TRUTH

Each of us has a map of the world inside our own minds. This map is literally shaping the way in which we perceive reality. No two people share the same map, as it is a unique creation based on our own personal beliefs, values, and life experiences. This map is constantly filtering our view of reality. The most important question is not whether your map is true; we know it can't be. What matters? Is your map useful, given the life you want to create? Does your map help or hinder you inside of what you're committed to fulfilling? Great news story here. You can expand and recreate the parts of your map that don't serve you. New map, new experience of life, and new results.

Wisdom #4 – Gratitude Transforms Life

There was a time in life that I was ungrateful for what I had. Based on my own self-image, I was never enough, and so none of the things I created were enough. This lack of gratitude meant I was blocking abundance from manifesting in my life. We will never gain more if we aren't grateful for what we already have. No matter the circumstances of our lives, we can ALWAYS find something to be grateful for. Gratitude increases your capacity for love of self and others, improves your experience of life, and improves your ability to achieve your goals.

Wisdom #5 – Make Personal Growth a Lifestyle

There is nothing to fix about you! I am going to say that again. There is NOTHING to fix about you. Each of us has things about ourselves and our lives that don't work; that's not the same as saying that you are broken or in need of fixing. I invite you to look at a journey of self-discovery and personal development as an opportunity to level up your life ongoingly. Human beings are living beings, and as such, have an inherent desire for growth. Start today with whatever resources you have to set goals that cause expansion. Study materials, books, and individuals who are a gap for you and invite you to discover what's hidden from your view.

Wisdom #6 – Serve From the Overflow

I will never forget being 14 years old and getting a call from my mom's best friend. I was going through a tough time, and I am not sure what she sensed, but she reached out to offer her support. She told me that until I learned to love myself, I couldn't fully accept the love of others. It took me decades to understand her words. Now, I know that you can't serve others from a cup that's empty, nor can you acknowledge or receive the love of others until you love yourself. None of us is perfect; we all do things that work and don't work. When you can embrace yourself without any invalidation for the parts that don't work, a whole new experience of life becomes available. Taking care of you is an act of self-love that will create abundance for all around you. When your cup is full, you can ongoingly serve from the overflow!

Wisdom # 7 – Anyone Can Be a Leader

Being a leader is not a function of your title or position. Anyone can choose to be a leader in their own life. Leadership is a function of who you are, and the actions you take. Leaders take responsibility for their lives. Leaders create win-win outcomes for all, lead by example, and ensure that the entire team is taken care of. Look in your life and do an honest assessment of the areas where you show up as a leader and those you don't. Now, you might not want to take the lead in all areas of life. There is nothing wrong with empowering others to share the load. Just make sure that you are sharing leadership, not deferring.

Wisdom #8 – Ask Quality Questions

One of my incredible mentors, Danielle Amos, always says, "The quality of your life is given by the quality of the questions you ask!" What kinds of questions do you engage with? Do you ask why others have things that you want? Or why life isn't fair? Are you a victim of your circumstances, or are you in the driver's seat of your own life? The kinds of questions you ask will directly impact how you experience your life and the results you achieve.

The Reward

My own personal journey of transformation has led to many tangible results that have improved the quality of my entire life. It hasn't always been easy, and yet, I am so grateful for all the growth. I have built a successful business, serving incredible clients who are making a difference in the world. I am scaling my business to seven figures and have new opportunities to serve all over the world. I have created a powerful platform in my podcast, heard all over the world so that I can allow the incredible journeys of fellow leaders to be shared. I am living a completely created life, travelling to countries like Bali while still serving my clients and growing my business. I get to spend every day facilitating the greatness of female leaders out to transform life on this planet.

Power Summary

Let's recap some of the key points in this chapter:

- Fill in the blank. Self-love is_____!

- Why is it so important to inquire into what you authentically want for your life?

- What becomes available on the other side of falling in love with yourself?

Success Actions

- Start a daily gratitude practice. Start your day writing out 5 to 10 things you are grateful for in your life! End your day as you go to sleep thinking about 3 to 5 things you are grateful for from the day.

- Write out in specific detail the life of your dreams. The more detail, the better. Record yourself reading the life script in the emotion of how it will feel when you are living that life. Listen to your life script at least once daily in a meditative state.

- Build accountability, partnership, and structures for success around achieving your goals.

> *"When it comes to pursuing that which*
> *lights up your soul, LEAP! You have spent*
> *your whole life becoming ready for this*
> *moment!"*
> ~ Amber Howard

With Love and Gratitude,

Amber Howard

About the Author

Amber Howard is a leading expert in strategic business development and mindset. She is a highly trained consultant, coach, and facilitator. Her experience, expertise, and robust toolset have placed her in the forefront of the consulting industry, where she has transformed organizations through bridging their gaps and driving sustainable change. With over 25 years of experience servicing various industries, she took her extensive credibility and wealth of knowledge and created Amber Howard and Associates, whose sole purpose is to serve female leaders of socially conscious enterprises.

Amber's methods are innovative, focused on mutually beneficial outcomes, and designed to optimize the allocation of resources. She supports her clients by identifying their true needs, designing solutions that have her clients achieve their goals with velocity, and guides them every step of the way.

Contacts

Website: www.amberhowardinc.com

Podcast: www.whatwouldamberdo.com

Free Gift: www.amberhowardinc.com/worthygoalsebook

Facebook **Group:** https://www.facebook.com/groups/leadersforlifealways

LinkedIn: https://www.linkedin.com/in/amberlhoward/

Twitter: https://twitter.com/amberhowardinc

Instagram: https://www.instagram.com/amberhowardinc/

"Blow Up The Box" Problem-Solving

Angelica "Andie" Monet
Business Optimization Expert, USA

"No one can stop you, but you."
~ "Andie" Monet

My Nightmare

I was confused...scared...and homeless. I was only 16 years old. In an instant, I was homeless because my mom had abandoned me with no warning.

The day started with me getting up for high school; it ended with me sleeping in the streets. My entire life turned upside down. Now I only had the clothes on my back, literally – no food, no money, no car, no job. Whatever I needed to do, I had to figure it out on my own – and fast! Where do I sleep? How do I eat? For goodness' sake, where do I physically "go"? How would I earn money, and who would hire me? But for now, I ended up hiding and sleeping in bushes, laundry rooms, and under decks.

During the next month that followed, still homeless and going to school and feeling embarrassed, all I did was figure out a way to graduate high school (and not drop out), learn how to apply for college, find a place to live, and how to earn some money. Since I had never done any of these things before, it was all a new world. "Where" do I find any of these things? In "those days," there were no cell phones or Internet.

I feel lucky that I loved reading. I was often at the library until it closed, even before I was homeless. It was safe, quiet, peaceful, and full of information. There, the world was at my fingertips. Now, the library really became my "home" until it was time to find a place to sleep in the bushes. While there, I looked for ways to graduate high school early, learned how to apply to college, where to find a place to live, and how to find a job. The library was like "*Google*" in the flesh." And so, it wasn't long before I found answers to all of those questions.

45

Within a handful of months of my high school year ending, I had formally filed documents to graduate high school early, applied *and* was accepted into college, and applied for financial aid. I even enrolled in classes, being conscientious about taking early morning classes so I could still work during the rest of the day. I was finding solutions and getting things done! And I was still doing well in high school during all of this craziness. Yes, I was still scared, but fear would have to wait. There were more important things to do. But as quickly as I found solutions, I also found much opposition, constant and intense.

When the principal found out that I was planning on graduating early. He not only forbade me but also told me that it was not possible. I had begged my high school teachers to change my final exam dates because my first week of college was the same week as high school final exams. They said no. The college financial aid department disqualified me for financial aid. They said – get this – that "no one could live off of this so-called income, so someone must be supporting me." They would not give me financial aid unless my parents submitted their tax returns! When I told them my situation, they didn't believe me or didn't care. I don't know which. Either way, no financial aid for me. The planning and research were working, but clearly, the execution was not.

Light at the End of the Tunnel

To give you a small window into my thoughts, what I knew with all my heart and soul, without a question or doubt in my mind, even before I was homeless, was this:

- I would go to college;
- I would help change the world;
- I could figure out what I had to figure out.

Figuring things out, at that time, was not confidence or ego. It was out of necessity. And now I needed to rely on my ability to solve problems, which was "simply" a logical analysis: I couldn't start college if I was in high school, and I couldn't work full-time if I was still in high school. It was just a puzzle to figure out. So armed with my mindset of "gotta get it done," I ran headfirst into fighting, clawing, and knowing that I would find a way. Starting college and earning a living to survive was more than determination; it was a matter-of-fact expectation. It never occurred to me that I wouldn't accomplish this.

Within weeks of my high school year ending, I *did* formally graduate from high school at 16 years old. I *did* reschedule my final exams. I *did* finish high school with good grades. And I *did* start college at 16. Earning income, on the other hand, was more challenging than graduating high school and starting college. No one wanted to hire a 16-year-old. So, for my next problem-solving trick, I started my first business.

Finding My "Yes"

I went door-to-door asking businesses if they could use some help, any help – copying, bookkeeping, taking out the garbage, cleaning, answering phones during the receptionist's lunch break. But convincing people to hire someone at $1 to $2 per hour is not as easy as you'd think when they are faced with a 16-year-old, quiet, timid, soft-spoken, unrefined, unkept, homeless, minority girl. The journey of earning enough money to survive was a long, difficult journey, and there was no one to help me, no one to teach me, and no one to learn from. So, I just had to start problem-solving again.

Here's what I was working with. First, I asked if they needed help. I received a "no." Second, I told them how I could help. I still received a "no." I told them that I was a hard worker and dependable. Still "no." What *else* could I say? And finally I figured it out.

They often asked if I had experience. "No." But now, instead of *just* telling them "no," I also added, "but there's nothing that I couldn't learn." Ba-bam! I got my first "YES"! That was my first, and some of the most important, self-taught business lessons: be honest, be genuine, but also provide value by giving them an *excited* reason to say yes.

Within months of being homeless, I was just scraping by, but was making enough money to live *and* to pay for college. More significantly, with repetition and income came confidence. And with confidence came many more self-taught business lessons. Not only were these lessons learned by "just" problem-solving, but I believe, more importantly, by living in "ignorance." My lack of "knowing any better" made it possible to find solutions outside and beyond what society had determined was "normal." And within four years of being homeless, when I was barely twenty years old, I was now working with one of the most prestigious and globally known companies in the world and getting paid more than I had ever previously earned. This was all because of my looking outside the box that most people define as "possible" which I practiced, honed, and grew into something the was my own superpower.

Awakening the Warrior in Me

There was one particular day I remember with a client. One of the young ladies that I trained and managed realized that she forgot to do something that was now late. The young lady was in tears and begged me not to tell the owner. But I knew that was not an option. I went straight into his office and told him the situation. And you know what he did? Yes, he yelled at me. He yelled all the normal things: "Why! How could you! Why haven't you trained them correctly?" You name it. He probably said it. And what did I do? Nothing. I just waited…patiently. You may ask why I waited patiently, and my answer is simple: I was confident enough in myself and my work so his reactions did not affect me. But more importantly, I also realized after that incident that he respected me more and trusted me more. Why? Because he knew that I would do what's right even if it meant losing my client.

I "feel" many things about my childhood and challenges. But what I *"know"* is determining what to "do next," whether next in business or next in life, was a "simple" matter of understanding the problem, challenge, and constraints, and identifying, testing, and trying new ways to solve them. The eventual questions and answers added to my "toolbox" of running, managing, and building businesses. And those tools were in many areas, from "soft" skills like communication, values, and leadership to more "direct" solutions in marketing, operations, I.T., management, and finances. With tears, elbow grease, confidence, determination, integrity, and the passion to help others, I would help thousands improve operations and profitability, and even help them avoid bankruptcy.

My Unordinarily Ordinary World

My life was not "normal." Some people cannot identify with. But then again, there are parts that many people can. I had a single mother. I went to six schools between kindergarten and when I graduated high school. I didn't have a lot of friends because we moved around so much. I was socially awkward. I loved reading but partly read to escape to another place. I always followed the rules. I was afraid of my own shadow most of the time. I rarely saw my dad. And even though my mother was emotionally unavailable and physically abusive, she loved me. She taught me how to be strong. My grandmother taught me about consistency, love, and belonging. And my great-grandmother taught me that faith, respect, and the responsibility of doing the right thing were of the utmost importance. And all these followed me through the years.

What I also knew, as far back as I could remember, is that I would help change the world. I didn't know what that looked like or how I would do it. Maybe I would cure world hunger? Maybe bring peace during war? Maybe even lift under-developed countries to sustainable economic levels. I was open to all possibilities – maybe even more than one! It was such a deep "knowledge" that there was no question about it. I thought that I'd figure it out when it was "time," but life decided I would start sooner rather than later.

While I never expected that my mother would abandon me, I never stopped believing that I would still make a difference in the world. And over three decades later, I *have* made a difference. My life had eventually taken me from small business, to corporate, to helping develop 13 countries' economic and financial infrastructure. My mess became my blessing to others.

Eight "Blow Up The Box" Tips

Looking back on over three decades of business consulting, I have had one secret sauce that runs through it all: Whatever the challenge is, disregard the reasons and excuses and limitations.

If you keep coming up with reasons why a solution won't work, say out loud, "Why Not?" I think you'll find, if you dig deep that there isn't a *good* reason. For example, "Why *not* graduate early at 16 years old?" "Why *not* start college at 16 years old." "Why *not* start a business at 16 years old". You get the idea. This is how I first started to "Blow Up The Box". This box limits your success, your profits, and your future.

I now teach women how to increase their revenue and scale their business with little or no cost. I have many free webinars but also have courses for those who want more. One of my favorites is a 5-day course with tips, tools, and teachings to build revenue:

http://www.5dayBusinessBootcamp.com

"Blow Up The Box" is about breaking out of the mental limitations that we put ourselves in, society puts us in, or family and friends put us in. With "Why Not?" in mind, here are only a few out of several hundred ways that you can "Blow Up The Box" in your own business:

Wisdom #1: You do NOT need money to make money.

Yes, I understand that marketing, especially these days, costs money. However, money is an accelerator, not a requirement. I have taught many small business owners how to increase business and revenues without any additional costs.

Wisdom #2: You do NOT need to work 60 or 70 hours a week to be successful.

Yes, you have to fulfill client "orders," but if you're working more than 40 hours per week, you'd be surprised how many options you have to work "smarter," not "harder."

Wisdom #3: Data is not a dirty word.

How can you make better business decisions if you don't have any data to make those decisions with? If you're not capturing or identifying some key data points and indicators in your business, you could be losing 25% to 35% of your profits.

Wisdom #4: Hiring more people is not always a solution.

When your business is growing, it's very tempting to hire more people. In fact, this may not actually be needed. One of the first steps to becoming more efficient (and "create" time in the day) is to define processes and training systems.

Wisdom #5: Your financial statements do not just show profit and revenue.

They can provide so much information from identifying inefficiencies and knowing why you don't have cash in the bank even though you are showing a profit, to which products are losing money, and so much more.

Wisdom #6: Accrual, not cash.

Sorry ladies. If you're not running your business on an "accrual method" of financial reporting, I guarantee that you'll never grow your business. Sadly, but unfortunately, that's true.

Wisdom #7: Don't implement a new system.

Many people, prompted by software companies, will tell you that you need a new system (ERP, CRM, SaaS, etc.). While this *could* be true, many times, it is not necessary. You can get another two to five years out of your existing systems if you know how to optimize and maximize their "functionality." (Such a fun word?)

Wisdom #8: It's okay that you don't know something.

Many small business owners feel embarrassed about not knowing how to do something in their business. In fact, you are an expert at what you do, but typically not how to "run a business." Owning a business is a journey. So free yourself from the "Box" of having to know all the answers.

Through Strength Comes Blessings

I am grateful that I get to work when I want. More importantly, I get to NOT work when I don't want to work. I can stay home with my son if he's sick. I can visit my adult daughter if she wants help. I can help a friend for the day. I can take a month off during our annual summer vacation.

I have been on numerous podcasts, been interviewed in several magazines, wrote books, been on 16 radio stations, helped several Fortune 500 corporations, and have spoken with senior editors at *Forbes* magazine. I will be speaking on a *TEDx* stage, at the U.S. Air Force Academy, and at the U.S. Olympic training camp. And, God willing, I will be launching a youth camp to teach children about leadership, entrepreneurship, and life skills.

"Blow Up The Box" Problem-Solving

Money and prestige are not what drives me, though. They are only tools, tools to touch as many lives as possible. I know that I can be a blessing to people's prayers. Not only can I give people business solutions to the "crying on the kitchen floor with ice cream" moments, but I give them a restful night's sleep and good health from lack of stress and anxiety. I can give people a financially secure future. And most importantly to me, I can give people love, support, and guidance that some people do not have in their lives at all. I can be what I never had. And that fills my heart each morning.

My "changing the world" has come in so many ways, including bringing communities together and being part of a global economy of small business owners.

Power Summary

Before you go, I want to leave you with a few insights to remember:

- If you keep hearing yourself say "no" to a possible solution, ask yourself, "_____ _____?"
- When you have a challenge, make a list of what you have already tried. Then practice identifying "unusual" ways to solve it instead;
- The only one standing in your way of success is one person: – _____. (Hint: rhymes with "tea.")

Success Actions

Here are three success actions that you can practice to "Blow Up The Box" for yourself:

1. Write down your biggest challenge or fear about your business;
2. Write down 10 ways your business would change if this challenge was solved;
3. Create one "crazy" solution and say aloud, "Why Not?"

"Andie" Monet

It's not "Why Not?" It's "Why Not!!" Be deliberate about it! Believe it! It will free your mind and heart for new possibilities to come in."
~ "Andie" Monet

With lots of love and blessings to come,

"Andie"

About the Author

Angelica "Andie" Monet is a best-selling author, speaker, and Business Optimization Expert who has advised Fortune 500 companies, governments, and over 1,000 small businesses for over three decades in 22 industries and 10 countries. She has been featured in magazines, on stage, and in several podcasts.

Her passion is helping women business owners get the support and training they need to exponentially grow their profits and make confident and strategic decision making with her "Blow Up The Box" system.

When she's not training for triathlons or serving at her church, Andie can be found building her non-profit to support youth leadership and entrepreneurship, hoping her adult daughter, Amber, calls her sometimes and indulging in sci-fi and adventure movies with her son Luke, where they live in Texas.

"Andie" Monet

Contacts

Website: http://www.AndieMonet.com

Email: Andie@AndieMonet.com

Six Ways to have Explosive Growth in 30 days – Free Course:

http://www.AndiesFreeGift.com

Social Media

Instagram: http://www.instagram.com/andie.monet_ssd

Facebook: http://www.facebook.com/andie.monet.ssd

Twitter: @AndieMonet_ssd

LinkedIn: http://www.linkedin.com/AndieMonet-ssd

Attracting the Love

Emmy Hernandez
Love and Relationship Coach, USA

"If you yearn for Soulmate love, it is yours
to have in this lifetime."
~ Emmy Hernandez

The Meltdown

I woke up, for the third time in a row, to my pillow drenched in my own tears. My soul had cried all night, and I hadn't even noticed. "How the hell did I get to this point?" I thought to myself.

I was in Mexico on yet another business trip. By this point, I had spent most of the previous 12 months traveling and training tech entrepreneurs on launching their apps and getting funding from venture capitalists. I was a phenomenal coach, and I was asked to speak all around the world at different conferences and got paid to travel and stay in nice hotel rooms. At first, I loved all the traveling. And then... I hated it! I lived out of a suitcase and out of hotel rooms. I had no social life back home in San Francisco, and my dating life was non-existent.

And, oh yeah, another thing... I absolutely HATED myself for coaching my students the way I was taught. I was taught to be cruel and mean and a bully and to have no regard for public humiliation. I was taught how to coach in a specific methodology that worked really great for the old White men in Silicon Valley. And the truth is that it worked for me too, at least for a little bit. I am the eldest of seven children, so I was a natural-born "bossy pants." But something had been bothering me for a long time, and I knew something was wrong. I just didn't know what.

And this morning that I woke up to my puddle of tears was the third day. I finally listened. Something HAD to change.

My soul was YELLING at me to stop what I was doing! I was really good at coaching my tech entrepreneurs, but what I really enjoyed was seeing them grow and progress into a better version of themselves. The problem with this was that the methodology I had to follow did not permit me to help them as human beings. I was meant to treat them like robots. This meant that I had to be a very domineering, "masculine" presence always. And although my ego loved that level of control, my soul was quietly crying herself to sleep, night after night, until those tears were too unbearable to keep bottled up. My soul, or what I call my "feminine" presence, wanted to become a more prominent part of my life.

The next month, after I finished training that cohort of entrepreneurs, I decided to quit that industry and look for something that made my heart sing. I didn't know what I was going to do next, but the Universe has a funny way of lining that up for us when we're open to the possibilities. I had to be firm with my decision. When different organizations emailed me with enticing offers for a speaking opportunity or a new program, I had to respectfully turn them down and let them know that I didn't work in that area anymore. This is what I call creating "Sacred Boundaries."

The Turning Point

I decided it was time to quit Silicon Valley and Bay Area Living altogether. I had taken myself on a solo trip to Greece to celebrate my 30th birthday. Don't get me wrong, my trip was amazing, but I knew that deep in my heart, I had started to miss being away from my family, and my heart also yearned for true love. By this point in my life, I had already survived a crazy, toxic, narcissistic boyfriend for two years who had left me emotionally and financially bankrupt. However, I had built myself back up and was no longer living in depression, and I had regained my financial stability. No abundance yet, but at least I could pay my bills.

After a heartfelt conversation with one of my best friends in San Francisco, I knew that it was time for me to move closer to my family. That was a very difficult decision for me. I had left home when I was 17, and here I was now at the ripe age of 30, single, with no children, no new job prospects, and missing my family dearly. My family had relocated from Los Angeles to Omaha, Nebraska, and had been there for 10 years now. I would visit once a year for Christmas, but that was it. Now, I was uprooting my life to live in a new state and start a new life.

To be completely honest, I wasn't planning on staying in Nebraska long. My plan was to use Omaha as a temporary location to live before I could find a new gig in New York. But things changed once I got there…

Nine months after I arrived in Omaha, I met the love of my life, my

Attracting the Love

Soulmate, Matt.

And EVERYTHING changed for me, for him, for us!

The Impact

After I met Matt, for the first time in my life, I wasn't making decisions based on my next career move up the success ladder or the corporate ladder. I finally realized there was so much more to life than career success.

The first week Matt and I met, we were already discussing marriage, and two years later, we were engaged. I'd love to tell you all about our amazing relationship and romance, but that's not what this chapter is about. It's about allowing the Universe to let the stars align and stepping into your true life's purpose.

For many years before I met Matt, I had been doing the work to attract and manifest him. Once I did, many women wanted to know HOW I did it. I shared that with many close friends in confidence, but I never dreamed of sharing my journey publicly. Until, one day, at one of my temporary non-profit jobs that I was working at, I realized just how much I missed coaching people and seeing their faces light up with breakthroughs. I KNEW that I didn't want to go back to tech coaching, but maybe, just maybe, I could coach women on attracting Soulmate love too. At the time, it truly was more of a question and doubt in my mind than it was an answer.

The Truth Will Set You Free

I was too embarrassed to change my *LinkedIn* Profile to "Love Coach." *What would my Silicon Valley connections think of me?* I thought they would laugh at me and ridicule me. But something magical happened as soon as I switched my niche and created a new brand for myself. I started getting many women reaching out to me on *Facebook* and *LinkedIn* and sharing very private matters with me that they had never shared with anyone else before. They were telling me all about their career success and how they were proud of that yet felt like they were failures in love. I told them that I completely understood. I was exactly where they had been just a few years prior, and that I knew exactly how to help.

I put a small group of women together that had the same goal of finding love, and I launched my first program. That was only 12 months ago. And as the saying goes, "The rest is history!"

My coaching business has grown to $300,000 in revenue in that small time frame. I have even brought on a head coach to help with the number of clients. My business is now on track to close $1.2M in business in the next 12 months and to impact thousands of lives.

My success has opened up a world of possibilities for myself and for my clients.

I not only coach single women looking to attract epic, healthy love, I also coach couples who need help finding their way back to connection and passion, and I also coach women on how to launch their business organically and authentically build a sustainable business.

Just think, if I hadn't been courageous enough to do what was right in my heart and get over my ego worried about my "title," I wouldn't be getting so many testimonials today and so many pictures of my happy couples.

I know that what I do now is my soul's purpose. I will be doing this work until my dying breath.

The Ordinary World

I am the proud daughter of immigrant parents from Mexico. My parents had nothing when they came to this country, and they built an empire for themselves and our family without ever having had the opportunity to finish elementary school.

I truly am in awe of my mother and father. They were the TRUE brave ones. They came to a new country without knowing the language or the customs and with no money. I can't even imagine how scary that must have been for them.

I am a proud big sister to six siblings. They have all been my greatest mentors. Thanks to them, I learned patience, kindness, and nurturing. I wouldn't be who I am today without my family, and I'm grateful for all the fights I had with my mom when I was a teenager. I learned very early on in life how to stand up for myself and speak my truth.

Guess what, mom? I get paid A LOT of money now to talk a lot out loud. Hehe Hehe!

So funny how the skills and tools we accidentally pick up when we're young become our greatest attributes as adults.

My mom saved my life a countless number of times when I was in danger. When I was seven. I developed a crippling anxiety disorder and created intense physical pain in my abdomen. When I was 16, my mom took me to a specialist to find out what was happening to me. My digestive tract had completely halted for two months, and I was very, very sick. My mom was desperate for answers. At 16, I had my first endoscopy, and my doctor told me that I was allergic to my own intestines and that I would live out the rest of my life with very bland foods and a heavy regiment of medication. I went off to college the next year and never saw that doctor again.

I went off to UC Berkeley, and when I was about to graduate, I had another endoscopy. My symptoms had only worsened under the stress. I was now 20 years old, and I was in pain as long as I was awake. I was taking up to 20 pills a day to attempt to mitigate the pain. And then I started waking up in pools of my own blood. I was bleeding to death in my sleep due to the pills because they were anticoagulants. I knew something had to change, but after my endoscopy, my doctor merely stated that I should keep doing what I was doing. There was nothing he could do to help. Mind you, he thought that I was ONLY taking four pills a day. So, I said nothing and continued on with my life.

Four years later, after a scary car accident, I was introduced to Dahn "Energy" Yoga in order to help alleviate my lower back pain. Three months after following their routine, my back pain had completely subsided, but even better, my stomach symptoms were 99.99% GONE!

From them I learned the power of meditation, intention, and energy from the Universe. I also learned physical exercises that I still use to this day.

I still get random flare-ups every once in a while, but this is now 10 years later!

I am very grateful to the leaders of Dahn Yoga for giving me my life back. I no longer live in physical pain and can actually travel and go entire years without having to take even one pill.

Power Summary

Let's recap some of the key points in this chapter:

1. Once I stepped into my truth, how long did it take me to make $300,000 in my Love Coaching Business?
2. Why is it so important to listen to your body?
3. What is your best guess as to what would have happened if I continued doing a job that my soul hated?
   a. Ended up in the hospital with "burn out" or adrenal fatigue?
   b. Lived happily ever after?

Success Actions

Here are three Success Actions that you can do to help you attract the epic, amazing love that you yearn for:

1. Register for your FREE Mini-Course to Attract Soulmate Love at the end of this chapter. My gift to you! You're welcome! ☺
2. Commit to doing the Soulmate Meditation Daily and DO IT! (Meditation is found inside the Soulmate Mini-Course)
3. Go buy an anniversary card from the store and write a card to your future Soulmate with a future date.

"Magic can only happen when you create
the moments of silence and self-reflection."
~Emmy Hernandez

xoxo,

About the Author

Emmy Hernandez is an executive-level love and relationship coach, international speaker, workshop facilitator, and author. After starting her consulting career in the San Francisco tech world providing services for companies like Lyft and Microsoft, she noticed a longing from women and couples who wanted to co-create an epic, passionate, and fulfilling romantic partnership but did not know how to do it. This was the catalyst to Emmy's private practice.

Emmy is also the author and host of "Ask Emmy Anything," a regular column published in Arianna Huffington's "Thrive Global," dedicated to answering your questions about love, Soulmates, and romantic myths. Fluent in both English and Spanish, Emmy speaks at conferences, organizations, businesses, and universities all around the world. Emmy graduated from UC Berkeley with a degree in Communications and is certified in NLP (Neuro-Linguistic Programming), Superconscious Recodes, and Male vs. Female Brain communications.

Emmy Hernandez

Contacts

Website: https://www.dualityofathena.com/

Email: emmy@dualityofathena.com

FREE Mini Soulmate Course:

https://bit.ly/FreeMiniSoulmateCourse

Social Media

*Facebook***:** https://www.facebook.com/emmyhernandezcoach

*LinkedIn***:**

   https://www.linkedin.com/in/relationship-coach-communication-coach/

*Twitter***:** @emmylovecoach

*Instagram***:** https://www.instagram.com/lovecoachemmy/

Forgiveness

Gaby Puma
Shaman and Transformation Guide and Coach, Peru

*"You are always One Choice Away from
Changing Your Life!"*
~ Mac Anderson.

The Meltdown

"What yet is UNFORGIVABLE for you, Gaby?", my mentor asked me.

After a long pause, and with my sacred tears now streaming down my beautiful face, "It's my parents," I replied. My heart couldn't believe what I had just said. I thought to myself, REALLY? After all the inner work I have done, and I am doing?

I didn't see that truth coming!

As a little indigenous girl at the age of six, I would walk a mile or two to collect water. It was my responsibility to collect it correctly and quickly. If I would spill any of the water on the way home, I knew that I would be punished, and the belt or whip would be taken to me. Sometimes the water would spill because of the challenging trail I had to walk. When it would spill, my body would recoil in fear knowing the punishment I would receive when I get home for not completing a job well done.

Then, on a certain day when I was at the spring's edge collecting water, a family friend snuck up behind me, grabbed me, and took me up behind the trees at the spring's edge. He put his hand over my mouth to silence me, and he then violated my innocence and raped me. After he finished his dehumanizing assault on me, he told me not to tell anyone about it. Stumbling back home in shock, hurt, and feeling ashamed, I arrived home with the water late, which instigated even more lashings.

Despite the lashings, I never told my parents what had happened. I kept this secret to myself. His horrendous abuse silently continued when my parents would unknowingly leave me under the care of his family whenever my parents would be away from our home, not knowing they were leaving me with a monster.

The trauma of sexual abuse didn't end there. It also came from other community members who would touch me and molest me whenever they had the opportunity, and I became further detached from myself, hoping and praying that someday this pain would end.

Following the years of emotional, corporal, and sexual abuse came one of the most painful events for me to bear – my parents' divorce. What made it so painful is that on all the other past traumas, my parents were there for me. Despite the punishment and dysfunction, I felt I had a family. Now that the family was broken, so was I.

Looking to pick up my brokenness, I decided to take care of myself and made the bold decision at the age of 15 to leave my family home to live in the city on my own. My dreams were to see the world, earn a degree, and become wildly successful and wealthy.

The Turning Point

I was now 28 years young, residing in Sydney, Australia, living my dream life on the outside! Yet, something wasn't right inside of me. I suffered from anxiety, anger, resentment, fear, insecurity, jealousy, scarcity, stress, and depression. Something needed to change.

By the grace of God, I was led to my first online business and coaching program, where self-development was introduced to me for the first time. It was 3 a.m. on the 30th of April 2017. I was binge-watching the content, and a major self-realization occurred. I could clearly see the power of my old MINDSHIT that shaped me and created my life experiences from my old set of beliefs based on past early trauma. Now, it was time for me to make an empowering change and shift to my MINDSET that would allow me, for the first time, to acknowledge, accept, and experience life as it is, not as I have always wanted or expected it to be!

As I began my serious self-assessment, I saw my past with bright new compassionate eyes and a forgiving heart. I could feel my human experience that had been numbed for far too long with the many pills and medications prescribed for inner and external pains.

I started to cry; I vomited, and my body started to release all of the emotions. Of course, I had forgiven so much in life over the years, yet now, forgiveness has deepened and elevated in me. It has become my best miracle – my friend and partner to walk with me now, especially as I continue my path of forgiving my cruel past, myself, my parents.

My ever-awaited new breath of life was rushing through me. After all of the times when it felt that life was always against me, I had to now prove it differently. I was inspired to change the direction of my life by creating a new life as I ventured onto my entrepreneurial journey.

The Impact

I started feeling overwhelmed with my new way of being and seeing the world. A lot of my memories from the past, the very masterfully buried wounds in my subconscious, were now revealing themselves into the light. Now I have this unshakable self-belief that this is the time to sit through the painful wounds and not allow their power to overrule my life and my future.

The only way out is through!

So, I needed to take radical action and heal the wounds of my trauma with my parents because I secretly blamed them for my suffering. I never thought I would have the courage to talk to them about my cruel upbringing. I had been fearful of talking about this as I had planned to take this conversation to my grave, but I needed to do this now and for my path and process of self-healing and transformation. I needed to release all the past energy I had carried with me from when I didn't feel loved, heard, validated, or accepted.

I received clear guidance from the Universe that said, "You need to return home to Peru." With my absolute faith, radical trust, and my renewed unshakeable self-belief, I started to close my life in Australia and start my journey back to my home and family in Peru. I needed to dispel the clouds of doubt surrounding the many events which urged me to discover the deeper teachings and gifts that life's painful experience has brought me. I needed to sit through the powerful healing, raw, and vulnerable conversations with my parents.

The Truth Will Set You Free

Arriving back to home in the Andes mountains of Peru to my small community, mixed emotions bubbled up through me. Now everything seemed fresh, and for an instant, I painfully doubted myself. I said to myself, *Maybe I made a terrible mistake. Maybe I should have stayed in Australia and powered through to become even more powerful as I've always dreamt in my entrepreneurship endeavors. How is this going to serve me?*

But then a deeper voice guiding me said, "You are exactly where you need to be; trust the process and listen to your heart's truth!"

My family embraced me and nourished me, being very happy with my presence and all the wisdom I'd gained. This time, our visit was absolutely different than my regular sharing of "worldly adventures." This time, I voiced deep inquiries and needed answers. What followed put us all through the test of strength, trust, and safety, along with the most powerful healing and freeing process that we all had experienced in a lifetime.

Following our indigenous lineage of ancient traditions, we performed endless rituals and ceremonies for healing, for powerful transformation.

The levels of forgiveness and love for each circumstance that once I condemned my parents for were now freeing my truth and freedom. I felt blessed that both of my parents came together to walk every step of the healing process with me (remember that my parents are divorced). When they acknowledged and accepted my feelings and emotions, I felt seen, heard, and loved in a new way that I had never experienced before. The cloud of resentment was lifted off my shoulders, and my heart felt lighter. It is true the memories may not disappear, yet their love and admiration freed me like nothing else.

What surprised me the most is how much of my most sacred and beautiful upbringing and rites of passage have been blurred by the trauma and my painful suffering. The more I healed, the more I saw the side of my sacred upbringing. Now I'm able to access my deeper truth and my innate gifts from my true self, which reconnected me to my ancient wisdom and spirituality.

The Ordinary World

I grew up in the Andes of Peru, a beautiful country with rich culture, traditions, and sacred lands. My mom is a master weaver, artisan, and farmer. My dad is a professional driver who served in the military. I have three siblings, a nephew, and a sister-in-law. My most favorite memories when growing up would be the Sundays at grandma's kitchen where my extended family – my cousins, uncles, aunties amounting to over 20 people – would festively gather, create complete chaos, and would enjoy eating healthy, homemade, ancient foods. After the feast, we, the children, would play climbing the trees. The adults would play soccer by the road in front of our family house in complete fulfillment, laughter, and joy.

One of the most significant values that I learned growing up in the Andes is that family, wisdom, and education are important. I am the first generation from my mom's bloodline to have access to higher education, earning a degree in travel and tourism, which inspired me to travel to over 30 countries all around the world.

I was raised on a foundation of living integrally, consciously, and lovingly with life. My family and culture respected the wisdom of our ancient luminaries, and we practiced their enlightened ways daily. I didn't fully realize the richness of the wisdom I grew up with until I lived through the polar opposite way of life.

Our village was considered one large family where we see and respect everyone as a   mom, dad, aunties, uncles, and where communal and cooperative practices are a way of life. My village received multicultural travelers, and we would integrate and consider them as part of our global family. From an early age, I have always seen the world as a global community and was curious about other cultures.

Around the age of seven, I was so intrigued by a tour bus I saw that from that moment on, I wanted to know more about the international travelers visiting my village. While at the same time, my desire to share my ancient culture with these travelers had also begun. This is how my career of travel and tourism emerged from interacting with various multicultural visitors and serving as their guide and healer in my intercultural and spiritual trips. That's why today, I find that I can easily connect with anybody regardless of their background and culture.

In 2016, I quit my travel and tourism career, making the decision to live in a new continent, Australia, to pursue a relationship, start a family, and making a complete career shift. It was one of the scariest moments of my life moving to a new country, leaving my family and a secure job. There were so many unknowns and little did I know that I would be facing one the most painful and fascinating moments of my life.

The painful parts were hitting rock bottom, ending my relationship, and losing my job. Yet, the fascinating and uplifting parts were that I experienced a life-changing moment of personal realization, a connection with my true self, and was introduced to my hidden passion of entrepreneurship.

This amazing experience of personal renewal led me to leave Australia and go back to my home and community in Peru to up-level my inner self-healing. It elevated me in my path and revealing my truth.

It opened my heart fully. Once the healing started, it was very clear how all my past life and professional experiences came together, forming my intercultural background experience of Western cultures combined with my ancient wisdom and spirituality.

This is my gift and the main pillar in my coaching business, guiding entrepreneurs and visionary leaders back to their true selves, accelerating their self-healing, spiritual growth, and transformation.

Lessons and Words of Wisdom

When I reflected back on my life's experiences, I realized the moment when I decided enough was enough and that I was the only one in my own way giving power to my past. Once I accepted and took full responsibility for my life through radical forgiveness, I found my truth. In return, I found the fierce courage to have raw, open, and powerful conversations with my parents that ultimately unlocked and freed me further.

Once we live in the freedom of forgiveness and truth instead of judgment and falsehood, we shift from being the victim of our life to being the creator of our life. That allows our true self to live in its divine purpose where anything is possible. I was able to accelerate my entrepreneurship journey and launch my online soul-aligned business. Now, I serve and guide entrepreneurs and visionary leaders from around the world to accelerate their self-healing and spiritual growth process.

Book your FREE discovery call:

https://calendly.com/gabypumacoaching/60min

Knowing what I now know, I listed below the key lessons I have learned in my path towards soulful success. I pray that you will find your light and strength from my wisdom because you are worthy of true soulful success, wealth, and freedom!

Wisdom #1: Acknowledgement

How many times do we want to avoid seeing things as they are, believing that something will magically change or shift for you or for things in life to change? As painful as it might be, rather than continually ignoring it, it needs to be recognized and witnessed for true change to happen for you.

Wisdom #2: Acceptance

How many times do we say we are accepting, and it may just be with our logical mind, or just because society tells us to accept it and move on? Here, I am referring to the real acceptance – to sit through the discomfort and pain, to feel what life has been for you until you see clearly your deeper truth and start claiming your power back from the people or situations and become self-responsible.

Wisdom #3: Letting Go

Knowing that anything that has ever occurred to you, as painful or as beautiful as it was, is now in the past. Let go of all attachments. Have the courage to see things with new eyes, being in the present YOU are right now. YOU are not the trauma or the painful experiences. YOU are a whole being, free spirit, divine, unshakable, loving, and compassionate soul.

Forgiveness

Wisdom #4: Be Forgiven

It is obvious that more of us are waking up to the reality of who we truly are. The practice of forgiveness is essential to making peace with your past and whatever you encounter along your journey. You do not deserve to be carrying any negative energy as it does you no good.

Who and what are you forgiving right now? Release the negativity and transmute it to love, to who you truly are. Travel light in your life and business.

Wisdom #5: Hire a Coach, Mentor, or Guide

I was entering new territory as a spiritual entrepreneur. I had no road map, and I wanted faster results, so I hired a mentor and followed in their footsteps. What's great is that my mentor is involved every step of the way, rooting for me and guiding me while I focus on what matters the most. This elevates my confidence, builds my audience, and positions me as the expert.

Wisdom #6: Take Action

No matter how big or small, actions taken produce results and build your courage to move towards the life you want to create.

It doesn't need to be the perfect action. Be messy, make mistakes, learn, grow, and repeat.

The Reward

I am so grateful to be leading life with inner peace and enjoying the best nourishing relationship with my parents and family. It is very important and sacred to me. I envision our global family doing the same. I am so blessed to be the one who broke the intergenerational trauma in my family.

That has allowed me to open my heart again. I have found true love, and now I am in an interdependent, happy marriage with my soulmate. If you don't have anyone to share and enjoy the beautiful life of success, freedom, and wealth, then what is the point, after all? You deserve it all!

I was inspired to give back to my community. I have created "AYNI Sponsorship" to help indigenous girls see and grow their role as global citizens.

This has reconnected me to my undying passion and purpose of helping people worldwide heal, transform, and accelerate their spiritual growth and realign to their purpose through my coaching business.

It has helped me open doors otherwise impossible for me, like co-authoring this extraordinary book, which will allow me to advance and grow my impact and share my message of elevating our human consciousness through living in forgiveness, freedom, and love.

It has helped me to reverse an excruciating autoimmune dis-ease. Rheumatoid arthritis.

When you find the courage and let go of all the burdens and the painful past, forgiving yourself and others, a whole new world and life are revealed to you where miracles are inevitable. I watch time after time this being true for my clients when they walk through this process. They are able to receive the love of their lives, create more wealth, and feel whole and free!

Power Summary

Let's recap some of the key points in this chapter:

1. Fill in the blank. Forgiveness will reveal your_____.
2. What was the radical action I took to start healing my trauma?
3. What was the wisdom hidden in the trauma for me?

Success Action

Here are three Success Actions that you can do to help you be soulfully successful.

1. Forgive yourself; stop being hard on yourself. The past is gone. Release the energy. Move forward towards the life you are here to create and lead.
2. Forgive others, make the call, have the courageous conversation, write a letter, write the email or message. Release that energy and reclaim your power back!
3. After forgiving yourself and others from this space of nothingness, you are vibrating at the highest frequency of freedom, love, and abundance. So, get ready to receive all the abundant and inevitable miracles of life!

Forgiveness

*"The weak can never forgive. Forgiveness is
the attribute of the strong!"*
~ Mahatma Gandhi.

Love & Light,

Gaby Puma

About the Author

Gaby Puma is an Andean Shaman and Transformation Coach who lives in California with her beloved husband, Mark.

She especially loves helping women entrepreneurs and visionary leaders reignite themselves into their own sense of power and purpose. Her greatest joy is seeing women growing their confidence in themselves and creating the best possible future for themselves and their families.

Gaby loves reading, playing, and being in nature.

Contacts

Website: www.gabypuma.com

Email: gabypumacoaching@gmail.com

FREE Strategy Session:

https://calendly.com/gabypumacoaching/60min

Social Media

Facebook: https://www.facebook.com/gaby.l.sallo

LinkedIn: http://linkedin.com/in/gaby-puma-b056a638

Instagram: @gabypumaglobal

Rules Not to Follow as a Woman Who Thrives

Jessica Fox
Master Transformational Coach, USA

Thriving in life starts by giving yourself
permission to embrace the ambitious woman
within
~ Jessica Fox

"Have you considered just focusing on being a mom for a while? You can always come back to this when your kids are older. I was talking to so-and-so about you, and they said the same thing. Maybe it's time you should let go of all these things you want to do and focus on raising your kids."

These words cut through me like a hot knife in butter. Was I hearing her correctly? Did she just suggest that I put aside my goals and dreams to "just focus on being a mom?" I sat there in stunned silence. This trusted leader, mentor, and friend, someone I had spoken to regularly about my dreams and ambitions. The person who was safe to admit that giving up everything for motherhood wasn't something she desired and had admitted she had gone on her own journey in needing to follow her sense of purpose and career while raising her kids is inviting me to let go of my dreams for "traditional" domesticity?

I couldn't have felt more betrayed. The one person I thought I could count on to believe in me and help me navigate the huge sense of purpose and dreams I held was not only talking about what I "should be doing" with someone else but no longer supported the dream, vision, and desires I had for my life and future. The grief that settled on my heart at that moment was profound, and I found myself alone and unsupported in my life goals and journey.

Have you ever experienced a moment like this in your life? Where the person or group that you thought understood you, that you openly shared your hopes, dreams, and struggles with, rather than support and encourage you to fulfill those dreams, suggested a list of *shoulds* and *shouldn'ts* that, in their opinion, are in your best interest? These *shoulds* are meant to guide you to the best outcome, yet these opinions have the opposite effect, leaving us questioning our judgment and doubting our ability to thrive and create the life we desire.

It's Because "Should" is a Shame Word.

The definition of "*should*," according to the *Oxford Languages Dictionary*, is: "to indicate obligation, duty, or correctness, typically when criticizing someone's actions." When we are being advised that we "*should or shouldn't*" do, think, say, be something, we are being told that the action, thought, word, or choice isn't correct, and we must change. This is why *should* has such a powerful ability to make us question our decision-making and make us feel like we are doing something wrong or foolish, which, by definition, is what shame is. And far too many ambitious and trailblazing women have felt the sting of *should* throughout the years, silencing many of us into submission to the status quo.

My first memory of feeling shame for wanting more of myself was at the age of six. I was sitting in church, listening to the preacher, and I knew that I wanted to be able to preach one day. I wanted to speak and help people every week, just like the pastor did. I remember turning to my mother and boldly declaring, "Mom, one day I am going to be a pastor and preach every Sunday."

My declaration was dismissed without discussion or discovery. Simply: "You shouldn't think like that. Girls can't be pastors."

Not being old enough to understand nor deconstruct dogmatic belief, the little, six-year-old version of myself internalized the shame of this statement to mean: "What is wrong with you? Don't you realize that because you are a girl, you aren't good enough?"

This memory is so distinct because this was where the thread of shame, which tied itself both to my desires and dreams but also to my femaleness, began its long and painful journey. I dealt with this shame by developing a drive to prove myself at every turn. I made it a point to prove to myself and the world that if a man could do it, I could do it better. But I also developed an internal terror at even the slightest hint of failure because I couldn't face not being good enough at something. And therefore, if I could not master something the first time I tried it, I quit rather than learn to develop the necessary skills to succeed. And that is when the big dreams I once carried as a child began to drop off one by one because the pain of failure was too great for me to carry because failure was just another nail in my "not-good-enough" coffin. And after nearly 30 years of operating like this, my body, mind, and soul could no longer keep striving, and I collapsed under total and debilitating burn-out that forced me to retire at 34 years old.

And that Changed EVERYTHING!

It was burning out and being forced to retire and go on disability that allowed me to finally look and see what was going on in my heart and mind. It was literally losing my ability to do anything that caused my striving to prove my worth to come to a sudden stop. There was nothing left to prove because I couldn't even get out of bed, and this is where the road to recovery started, and it began with deep and profound soul searching.

I began to recognize the patterns of fear that had been ruling my life up to that point. That fear is what drove me to success. I was fortunate enough to have a wise counselor teach me that living from and being motivated by fear keeps a person in survival mode because the brain is subconsciously always looking for danger. By no longer being able to perform and strive, not only was I able to give my internal survival center a much-needed rest, but I also finally had the opportunity to ask myself what it was I truly wanted for myself and my future. And the answer was clear, I wanted to learn how to live life from a place of thriving, not surviving.

And so, I began to learn to change the rules of *should and shame* that I had been living under. As I began to understand that my worth and value lay not in what I do but in who I am, and started making decisions in my life around who I wanted to be, the life I wanted to create, and the dreams I wanted to pursue and follow. With time, I started to unpack and let go of some of the most shameful *shoulds* that I had become, almost like rules that I had to follow. Each time I rejected the rule, the shame of it no longer held power over my life, and in return, freedom, joy, confidence, and growth replaced it.

The *"Should"* Rules Not to Follow

This list is by no means exhaustive, but these were some of the primary *shoulds* that I needed to come to terms with and let go of so that I could truly start thriving in my life. As women who lead and women who thrive in this life, awareness of our subconscious limiting beliefs or rules allows us to begin transforming those beliefs and grow into the next, more powerful version of ourselves. As you read this list, allow yourself to become aware of the *shoulds* that you hold and give yourself permission to let go of any fear or shame that still has power over you.

1. You Should Always Heed the Advice of Those Who Love You

Let me be clear, I am not saying to completely disregard the loving advice and insights of those closest to you. What I am saying is that you get to weigh any advice that comes to you and accept or reject it, no matter its source. When the advice doesn't land right and induces those feelings of shame or fear, it's important to pay attention to the response you are having because it indicates that their advice is not in alignment with what you know to be true about yourself and your future. Most people (in healthy relationships, that is) that love us are well-intentioned and only want what is best for us, but can often be clouded by their own experiences, biases, fears, and judgments projected toward us in the form of advice. When it comes to advice, we get to "Eat the meat and spit out the bones," as one of my mentors used to say.

2. You Should be Happy and Content with What You Have

This sentiment has often fallen on the ears of the ambitious visionaries, those who have huge dreams and desire to see incredible things in this life and in this world. In those moments when you know you are on the edge of a breakthrough in your life and the discontent of not yet having the missing piece to grow you to your next level, a little voice inside of you, and at times, people around you say, "You shouldn't be discontent, you have a great life, family, career, etc." I want to point out here that happiness and contentment are not linear. They are not a one-time status to be achieved and then maintained. Rather, that a healthy person is always growing and expanding from the inside out is a sense of discontentment that creates a desire and motivation to change and grow into the next amazing version of ourselves.

3. You Should Be a Traditional Domestic Mother as it is what is Best for your Children

And here we are, back to where this chapter began. What is "best for your children" is for them to have a happy and fulfilled mother and whether or not that looks like traditional domesticity is beside the point. Thriving means that you get to choose how you live out the different roles in your life in a way that makes you feel happy. You get to choose what is right for yourself and your family, whatever that looks like. If you are happy and fulfilled as a traditional housewife, amazing! If you are happy and fulfilled in your career, spectacular! If you are happy and fulfilled working from home, superb! Give yourself permission to be the woman you desire to be, recognizing that motherhood is a beautiful role within the whole context of your entire personhood, and when you choose joy and fulfillment, your children will truly get a mother at her best.

4. You Shouldn't Be Ambitious

Ambition in women has been given a bad reputation. It has been characterized as competitive, selfish, unfeminine, catty, and even unhealthy. Yet, the women that have changed history and inspired us in so many ways were ambitious. You get to change the narrative and understand that your ambition is amazing and sourced from feminine beauty. As Aine Kerr, COO of Neva Labs and Sulzberger Fellow at Columbia University said: "Sure, there have been massive challenges and sacrifices along the way – I'm now of the belief that anything a man can do, a woman can also do while breastfeeding. But I'm convinced that if ever you want something done, ask a busy woman. Yes, we're unapologetically ambitious, but we're fundamentally ambitious for our fellow citizens, our families, our friends, and the future generations we're here to nurture and inspire."

So, Let Go of the *Should...*

...and unapologetically create the life that you desire. Life is not "one size fits all," and the secret to thriving is taking responsibility for your own happiness and making your decisions from a place of alignment with the woman that you have been created to be. This is your invitation to fully embrace your dreams, goals, ambitions and do the work to overcome the limiting beliefs that are holding you back from your full potential.

As I have navigated the journey from living in fear and survival mode to thriving in my life, letting go of those "*should* rules" I held and the cycles of shame I lived, I have learned some valuable lessons that, with your permission, I'd like to share with you.

1. Professional help is a God-send. When we are in the thick of shame cycles, it is hard to see the thought and belief patterns we hold, some of which we may have been carrying since childhood. Someone who is impartial and willing to give honest and compassionate feedback as you navigate these beliefs is crucial to help us identify and shift our habits. It could be a professional therapist, counselor, or coach. It is someone who has been trained and has a proven reputation to help people overcome cycles of shame and limiting beliefs.

2. Life is cyclical, not linear. In terms of life and the personal growth journey, it is one of the peaks and valleys because we are ever-evolving and growing. It is the constriction in life, the discontentment, and frustration with our present state that provide the necessary motivation to change and grow into the next version of ourselves. When we shift our expectations about our life experience to understand that there are highs and lows, we are less conflicted in the low seasons because we understand that the struggle we are facing is an opportunity for us to grow. Where can you shift your expectations about your life experience, have grace for yourself in your circumstance, and allow yourself to learn and grow through the process?

3. Take responsibility for your own happiness. Allow peace, joy, freedom, and confidence to be your guide when making decisions. Trust your intuition and be honest with yourself about why you are making the choice you are making. I'm not suggesting a selfish approach to life because sometimes a responsible yet fulfilling life requires personal sacrifice. My encouragement here is to no longer make decisions based on a sense of duty or *should;* instead, taking an honest look at your decisions. A great question to ask yourself here is: "Does what I am saying yes to give me peace, and is it in alignment with my highest self and the life that I desire to create?"

Women who lead and women who thrive are the creators of their own life and legacy. They get to let go of the "rules" that do not serve them and create the rules that do! Your dreams, wants, desires, and ambitions are worthy of your time and attention. Giving yourself permission to thrive and define life by your own terms is acknowledging your inherent, divine worthiness, and it allows you to live from a place of love and joy. Actions and ambitions motivated by love and joy are powerful creators of an incredible legacy that can teach women in generations to come what a living a life fulfilled and free can truly look like.

Will you join me? It's time to rise and thrive!

Rules Not to Follow as a Woman Who Thrives

"Being ambitious is about being your own driving force – it's about having that inner belief and that drive – and that ebbs and flows throughout your life. To have ambition is a gift. It's a beautiful thing to have a goal, to reach for something and get it."
~Anne-Marie Tomchak

Good luck on your journey!

Jessica Fox

About the Author

Jessica Fox is blazing a trail for ambitious women.

You may have caught her on NBC, CBS, FOX, and The CW. She is a master coach, international bestselling author and has been interviewed on TED.

Jessica has worked with organizations such as the Flames NHL Hockey team, the Stampeders Canadian football team, Subway, and Starbucks.

Jessica has thousands of hours teaching and training from the stage and in intimate settings.

She has helped ambitious women hit consistent $10k sales months, go from laid off to signing a six-figure contract within three months and produce $53,000 in team sales in the first month working together.

Most days, you will find her in her comfiest jeans or yoga pants, enjoying good coffee and lost in her never-satisfied book addiction.

Originally from Canada, Jessica makes her home in northwest Arkansas, just a few miles from Walmart's headquarters, with her husband Tyler and their three amazing children.

Contacts

Check out my NBC feature here: https://bit.ly/3gHKqHF

Check out my *TED-Ed* feature here: https://bit.ly/3lb2FFr

Book your Free Pathway to Thrive Breakthrough Session:

https://bit.ly/consultjessfox

Website: www.happyandfreetobeme.com

LinkedIn: www.linkedin.com/in/jessicafoxcoaching

Instagram: https://www.instagram.com/heyjessicafox

Email: jessicafoxcoaching@gmail.com

The Change and Rise

Madison Marshall
Birth Doula/Student, USA

*"It takes more energy for you to continually
make excuses for yourself than to actually
go out and do what needs to be done."*
~ Madison Marshall

The Meltdown

"School will be in recess until April 20th, the week after spring break, due to the sudden outbreak of coronavirus."

This message echoed through the intercom while I sat at my desk in my 5th period advanced literature class surrounded by my senior classmates. Low chatters turned into cheers as we all realized that our final school year would be cut short and graced with a month-long spring break. I joined in on these celebrations, utterly ignorant to the fact that this "long spring break" would lead me to one of the lowest points of my life.

I shuffled through the crowds in the quad, making my way to the natatorium to pick up my swim backpack in my locker and head home. To no surprise, the celebrations continued on the pool deck after news spread that our swim meet scheduled for later that afternoon would have to be canceled. I was dreading swimming the four by one hundred relay, so I had no objections to the festivities even though I was expected to be devastated at the news as the team captain. After months of 5 am practices, late-night study sessions to maintain my 4.0, Thursday afternoon internship shifts at the birthing center, and teaching endless swim lessons to toddlers at the YMCA, I was overwhelmingly relieved to have a break from it all in quarantine. I had been blessed, more like cursed, with all the free time in the world, with no expectations, nowhere to be, and no more responsibilities, for a month, that is,

85

or so I thought.

The first week was utter bliss. My day started at 11 am when I casually rolled out of bed, dragged my feet to the kitchen to make a large cup of coffee and something sweet to satisfy my taste buds. After prepping my feast, I made my way back to bed to binge-watch feel-good comedies. 12:30 pm hits, time to head back to the kitchen for a mid-movie snack. Around 2 pm, I'm feeling creative and decide to scroll through Pinterest to find a unique cookie recipe to craft up back in the kitchen. While those are in the oven, I browse social media to stimulate my brain. After a few hours of munching on cookies and being held captive to my Instagram feed, the clock strikes 6, and I'm programmed to wonder, "what's for dinner?". I clean up the dinner plates, sigh, and think to myself, "it's been a long day; I deserve some dessert." It's almost 11 pm, I'm sitting in bed watching yet another rom-com, craving a midnight snack, and looking forward to another day just like this one tomorrow.

"Can you turn down the AC?"
I plead from the back seat sitting there with my green and yellow cap on, my green gown folded on the seat next to me. I reach down to open my window to get a better view of my drive-thru high school graduation but end up accidentally catching a glimpse of the rip around the buttons of my jeans where I had struggled to button them earlier that morning. As I glare out the window at posters that brightly state, "congrats, class of 2020," I think of my thirteen years of education and a promise that the thirteenth year would be magical. A promise that all my hard work would finally feel worth it once I'm standing up on the stage in my cap and gown, receiving my diploma in front of all my loved ones. But to my surprise, there I was, sitting in the back of my mom's SUV contemplating these broken promises. I wave a final goodbye to my high school teachers from the back seat as we cruise through the quad and I fear that they will notice the added weight in my face.

My daily rituals continued through the months of summer and halfway into my first semester of college until I found myself standing in the mirror, 50 pounds heavier and stripped of all motivation. Outside my bedroom where I spend the majority of my days, stress builds throughout the house as my family prepares for the arrival of a baby girl in mid-November. Back in my room, I'm chained to my desk as my professor's sharp eyes pierce me through our zoom chat room as he confronts me about my eight missing assignments and failing grade. I can't help tuning out to his lecture to tend to my inner excitement for the party I would attend later that evening to distract myself from the responsibilities in my life. I continually found distractions to keep me from what mattered and made excuses until I eventually ran out of excuses.

The Change and Rise

The Turning Point

The cool November sun shines through the sliding glass doors and the sparkles off the water in the birthing tub as I pull her up out of the water and place her on my mom's chest. We anxiously wait for her first gasp for air that will be followed by a sigh of relief and cries of joy that will fill our living room. I hold her close to my chest, and some of the sticky vernix rubs off on my hands, I take a breath, and it sets in that I have a new sister. I think what kind of example I want to set for her and quickly come to realize that the life I'm leading right now is not one that I want her to look up to. The lifestyle that I had become accustomed to over the last few months no longer just affected me but also took a toll on my family. I needed to be better not just for myself but for them.

I rummaged through my drawers at 6 am to find my workout clothes. I pull them out from the back of the closet and blow the dust off. They stare at me with excitement as they have been yearning for use for months.

"Ready to get to work?"

Without hesitation, I confidently say yes as I stand in the middle of the gym floor and wrap my brain around the set that my trainer Chuck scribbled out on the whiteboard. I knew the next 30 minutes would test my mental and physical strength, but I had hope that it would be worth it.

After about a month of forcing myself to stick to a tight schedule of waking up early, working out at least once a day, attempting to eat healthier, and staying on top of my school assignments, I finally saw some progress, but the work was not done yet.

"There's a Muay Thai Tournament in Arizona in April. I think you should do it."

Chuck explains this to me after he recently started incorporating kickboxing into my daily workouts at the gym to give me a better cardio workout. On the surface, the idea sounded compelling, and I knew that it would give me an extra push to lose weight and stick to a schedule because I'd have a deadline. The only catch: cut 40 pounds in 4 months, one challenge I was scared to but willing to take on.

The Impact

The second round ended with the bell and me falling onto my hands and knees in the corner of the ring while tears mixed with sweat streamed down my face. "I can't do this anymore" rang through my mind, but Chuck interrupted my inner dialogue when he yelled, "get up, you have one more round." I stumbled up off the ring floor to find my sparring partner standing in the opposite corner, barely wounded and anxious to go another round to finish me off. This fight was just practice; it wasn't even the real thing. Throughout my fight camp, I was tested mentally and physically time and time again. I developed a fear of failing, a fear that I was going to lose, and all my hard work would be for nothing. I came to understand that the only way I would stop the fear inside me was to face these fears head-on until I overcame them. I shut off the negativity replaying in my mind that told me I wasn't good enough and that I wouldn't fulfill my goal. I gripped my pen and wrote down every negative thought I had about myself during that fight camp. Once they were all down on paper, I wrote beneath it that I release these thoughts because they no longer serve me and my goals for my life. I felt in that moment the weight that these thoughts were holding on me immediately lifted off. This proved to me that if my mind was strong enough to take me to the edge of quitting something I was working so hard for, it, sure enough, would be strong enough to help me push through and finish what I started.

"Please step up on the scale."

I stood there in my Nike spandex and sports bra, fingers crossed, hoping I did enough to make weight. I couldn't help but let out a sigh of relief when I saw the man sitting at the table read the scale and write "135" on the paper. He looks up at me to say, "good job, you did it," and I feel myself wanting to cry and scream at the same time. I look up to thank him and walk off the scale; the most challenging part is over now I need to focus on the fight.

"And judge number 3 scores the bout 30 to 27 for your winner by split decision, fighting out of the red corner, Madison Marshall!"

The referee raises my left hand, and I hear the roar of the crowd. Did he say my name? Is this real? I was ushered to the podium in a daze to receive my trophy. I was in disbelief that I had done it. I trusted myself and my hard work, and it all paid off. As I gripped my trophy, I realized that a task that I would've deemed impossible a year ago finally became a reality. I knew I would never be the same and that this experience had changed me for life. I had wholly transformed myself mentally and physically to overall become a better person.

The Biggest Reward

My inspiration to work in the birth field comes from my mom, a doula herself, and truly sparked when I caught my baby sister. Natural birth is not a new phenomenon but is becoming more popular in recent years as women consider the risk/benefit relationship of a medicated birth. Many new and expectant mothers are researching their options to better their health and their baby's health. After conducting my own intensive research and witnessing the benefits firsthand through my clients, I am right there with these moms to advocate for their wants and needs in the delivery room.

Now, as I shift my focus from my self-transformation back onto my business in the birth community as an aspiring midwife, I still keep in mind all that I've learned about myself while training for my fight. In the past, I've had clients who were hesitant to hire me because I'm only 19 years old and have never had a baby of my own. They argue, "how can you truly know how to help me in my time of need if you don't know what I'm going through in labor?". This point is valid, but I've witnessed that birth is a lot like a fight from the births I have been part of. You go into it not knowing what to expect and scared for the outcome. It is one of the hardest things you can do to your body, it forces you to put your back up against the wall, and you must rely on your mental strength to get you to your goal. If anything, my fight experience allows me to relate to my clients in knowing what it's like to feel like you want to give up. Still, you have to train yourself to find your inner strength and push through the most challenging obstacles because it will all be worth it at the end of the day once you succeed.

I struggled the most in my fight camp when I noticed I was starting to plateau. I knew I needed to change something to keep excelling. At first, I resisted this change until I understood that the things we resent doing the most are going to be the things that will change the trajectory of our success. Once we get rid of our stubbornness to do what's hard, we can finally break through that ceiling onto the next level. This mindset pushed me to take the initiative to jump-start my business by taking on more clients by extending my outreach, getting new certifications that would make me stand out, and putting effort into my website and social media platforms. However, I'm still on my journey to success and learning along the way. I hold myself to the highest standard to regularly make leaps to become the best version of myself.

Success Actions

1. Find your why. Set your goal and commit to it.
2. Stop resisting change. Find comfort in being uncomfortable and embrace the change in your life.
3. Push yourself beyond what you think your limits are. Your mind is a powerhouse and you can do anything you dream of. Don't let anything get in the way of your dream.

*"Face the shadow of yourself and embrace
the change. It'll be worth it"*
~ Madison Marshall

Respectfully,

Madison Marshall

About the Author

Madison Marshall is a dedicated Doula and a Nursing student studying to become a midwife. Madison and her mother, Tiffany Turner, have built up their duo Doula services over the last few years and are constantly trying to expand in order to empower women through their birth experience. Madison is passionate about the birthing community and wants to aid the natural birth movement to change expectant mothers' perception of their birth and introduce new techniques to create a euphoric birth experience.

Contacts

Website: https://www.onpointbirth.com/

Email: MadisonMarshall252@gmail.com

Instagram: @onpointbirth

Grab the Opportunity

Michelle Mehta
Confidence Expert, USA

"Take a leap of faith with the opportunities
knocking on your door."
~ Michelle Mehta

Conquering My Fear

"Are you crazy?! Have you lost your mind?! What are you talking about?! You want me to do what?! A 40-Slide PowerPoint Presentation in front of 150 people, family, and friends?" I exclaimed on hearing the request.

This was nuts, I thought! I don't even know how to hold a microphone. What was I going to say; how will I sound? This is extremely nerve-wracking.

"Can't you do it, Dad? Why am I the one doing this? I don't want to!' I protested.

My dad encouraged me by saying, "Come on, Michelle, you can do it. It will be fun! Just follow the talking points, and it will be good. Don't worry!"

My dad's been my biggest encouragement, and he said that if I could do it, then I could do it! I practiced a few rounds. Thank goodness for my family's patience and the strength to believe in me as I practiced and felt more confident.

I was only 15 years old.

I only had one day to prepare. It was showtime, the day of my Sweet 16 Party was here. I was extremely nervous, excited, scared. I tried to be composed even though my stomach was in knots. I did not know what was going to happen at the end of the PowerPoint Presentation. All I knew was that I had no choice and had to deliver the best.

The DJ announced, "We will now have a PowerPoint Presentation, and the birthday girl, Michelle, will share a few words."]

Uh oh, that's me! Okay, here I go!

93

Michelle Mehta

With the microphone in my hand, I took a deep breath, and I launched slide after slide. Then, something magical happened! My nerves calmed down. I kept engaging with the audience, their smiles and laughter edging me on. Next thing I knew, the daunting PowerPoint Presentation was over.

Whew! I did it, and the audience loved it!

I realized that I conquered my biggest fear, the fear of public speaking, the audience's reactions, the judgment of myself, and most importantly, the judgment from family and friends.

I had no idea at the age of 15 that I was destined to be a public speaker. When I look back now, I was divinely guided in my curriculum through college that would give me the skills, not knowing that I would be a public speaker. I took a drama class in my junior year of high school and chose classes in college that forced me to do presentations that required public speaking. The skill sets that I learned included projecting my voice without a microphone and being able to use body language and vocal variety at the same time while sharing my message with the audience.

It took me 15 years before it dawned on me that I was going to be a public speaker on the world's biggest stage performing a *TEDx Talk.*

According to the National Institute of Mental Health, 75% of the world's population has a fear of public speaking, known as "glossophobia." There is still 25% of the population that has no problem speaking in public and can do it flawlessly. One does not know the fear until they experienced it.

When I was in drama class, I had no idea that this type of fear existed. I just did it for an ego boost of, "Wow, Michelle, that was excellent!"

I thought if they were complimenting me, I must be good at it. I went after the biggest fear of the world and made it my strength. As a result, I don't have any fear of public speaking.

It's Showtime

I attended California State University, Fullerton in California. One of my favorite pastimes became making announcements for the business courses. I became the voice of the finance department in the business school, announcing social opportunities on campus. I got to stand in front of an audience of up to 250 students. Everyone in the business school knew me because of my leadership role. I had no idea the impact I was creating with my messaging. All I knew was that I was passionate about sharing what the campus and the business programs had to offer. If a microphone was available, I would volunteer to share a few words no matter the occasion, just winging it. I was there, I stood up, I spoke out.

Who would have thought? I certainly didn't.

Grab the Opportunity

According to my parents' dreams, I was to go into selling financial services. They would be happy with banking products, insurance, or even recruiting – but not public speaking, let alone motivational speaking. But stubborn Michelle already decided that was what I was going to do!

I fell in love with promoting people to be the best version of themselves, not products or services. When I took a leadership and development course, I realized that coaching and speaking are where my heart is. This is going to be fulfilling for me and my dreams, not only being an entrepreneur, but also a motivational speaker.

Now, I had graduated, and it was time for me to get coaching on how to master my public speaking skillset, and the deeper I got into the coaching program, the more I wanted to have my message heard by the masses. I even had a brilliant idea to go Live on Facebook every week and share about leadership, coaching, and personal development. And so, I did under the brand of #ForwardingFridays and #FearlessFridays. After doing about 100 videos and having 1,000s of views, I decided to fulfill my dream of becoming the best I could be. I had no idea how that would be profitable or a successful career. I just wanted to inspire the audience to take the appropriate action needed to achieve their goals.

They Screamed TED!

I attended seminars, many seminars to help me be the best motivational speaker. Here I am at one, and I am asked to stand up and share my "WHY" out loud using the microphone.

I began, "I became a coach for teenagers to make this world a better place by providing confidence and motivation strategies. According to the World Health Organization, 61% of teenagers are suffering from anxiety and depression every single day in the United States, and 1,400 of those will attempt suicide. I knew what it was like to not have confidence and motivation in middle and high school. I wanted to be the voice and support system for teens to achieve success."

In 2019, I had the opportunity to do a presentation at a middle school in front of 100 sixth-, seventh-, and eighth-graders, 11 to 14 years old. I asked them a question: "How many of you have evil voices inside your heads?" Every single hand went up simultaneously. I then asked: "What are these voices telling you?"

Their responses were,

"I am not loved."

"I am not smart."

"I am overweight."

Where are these kids getting their thoughts from? That became my "Why."

I heard the coach ask the audience, "Where should Michelle share her message?"

They screamed, "*TED Talk!*"

In my head, I thought, Yes, for sure in 10 years from now when I am equivalent to a Brene Brown, a Bill Gates, or a Simon Sinek.

With the *TED Talk* seed planted in my mind, the next time I shared my "WHY," the event organizer was extremely convinced that I could do it. He offered a program to help speakers be the best speakers they can be and get on a *TEDx* stage.

I took a leap of faith and registered for the program. But my mind started screaming out loud, Am I good enough? Is my message worth sharing? What will my family think if I fail? What if my TEDx dream doesn't come true? What if there is no return on my investment?

I had to start the work by letting go of my own limiting belief of self-doubt and not feeling good enough. I needed to believe in myself and my passion for sharing my message.

During the program, I got my signature talk perfected for my niche of supporting teenagers to become confident and motivated to go after their dreams. After all I did, they can do it too.

The light at the end of the tunnel became brighter as the motivational speaker inside of me was slowly awakening.

Full Circle

I started my *TEDx* journey in May 2020 in the middle of the pandemic where things were shut down. My dream was alive and beating louder than ever. It was now time to prepare for my debut on the *TEDx* stage. A dream that I thought was 10 years away from now was soon to be a reality within a span of less than 12 months.

I couldn't believe that I was in this coaching program designed for people like me to be on the *TEDx* platform. I applied to five different places across the states and got selected at California State University, Fullerton (CSUF), the same university where I had spent five years of my life and where my dream of becoming a motivational speaker had started. FULL CIRCLE!

I got selected for the *TEDx* CSUF conference after my first round of auditions, and after six months of preparation, I was to become a *TEDx* Speaker.

A dream that has become a reality to last a lifetime! Oh my gosh, I am going to be on *TED*!

The Finale

It is 30 days before the *TEDx* Conference. Oh No! I had major rewriting to do as my talk did not meet the guidelines of the *TEDx* format. I had a 17-page speech that needed to be condensed to 1,700 words to be in the time frame of seven to nine minutes. How could I be my best version of the "best speaker ever?" It was the first time in my life that I was vulnerable enough to ask for support.

I reached out to the organizer and said, 'Can you please help me structure my talk? I am not sure if I have all the basics covered as I didn't even have a title."

Anybody that called me during the 30 days before the deadline would have to listen to my speech, share their thoughts and ideas, and help me navigate hand gestures, pausing, tonality, and everything in between to be able to present the best talk that I could. It was extremely challenging as we found out that we would be presenting in front of a camera from the comforts of our home without a live audience. This meant that I was the whole show. Thank goodness for my coaches, my experiences in public speaking, and shifting my belief system.

On February 12, 2021, the *TEDx* CSUF virtual conference was showcased via *Zoom* and *YouTube,* and I was the fourth speaker out of 11 speakers in the line-up. When I saw my performance on the big screen with my family and close friends, I could not believe that it was me. I literally felt like I won the Miss America Beauty Pageant. I had never worked so hard in my life.

My parents were extremely thrilled that I did not give up on my dream of being the best motivational speaker I can be on the world's biggest platform, the *TEDx* stage. I am now officially a *TEDx* Speaker.

YOU ROCK, MICHELLE!

No one can take that title away from me. It has branded me as an expert in my field and increased my own confidence in my personal and professional life.

Path to Success

When you really want something in life, and you truly believe that you can have it, the universe will create the opportunity for you, and all you must do is trust it, believe in it, and work hard to deliver it. It is very important that you focus on your personal "WHY" as to "WHY" you want to do it.

Now is the right time! I had many naysayers during my *TEDx* journey telling me that I should wait until the pandemic was over to deliver my talk. Set aside the voices in your head,

You do not have money in the bank to pay for it.

You are not credible enough to deliver something on this platform.

I am not good enough as other people who have given these talks.

…and eliminate any voices that do not support you. If I had listened to any one of them, I would have given up on my biggest dream.

"When the student is ready, the teacher appears." When you are ready, the coach that believes in you will show up. Ask for support when you need it. The *TEDx* organizers believed in my idea. I even asked them for support multiple times throughout the preparation, which a lone wolf, like me, would never ask for. You will be stretched out of your comfort zone, and you will need all the support you can get.

The opportunities will be amazing. IF NOT NOW, WHEN? I knew that if I didn't do it now, I would never do it. Despite the odds, set the intention, and make it a reality worth living and sharing. I am extremely grateful and blessed to be sharing this experience with you, and I have been proud of myself for taking the leap of faith of the unknown and making it a reality.

Knowing what I know now, I have been blessed to share my experience with female entrepreneurs in supporting them to share their message using the *TEDx* platform. As a result of being a *TEDx* Speaker, I am increasing my program offerings, pricing, and my business is exploding with more clients. The increased income and immense amount of pride and joy as I see my clients reach their goals and dreams every single day have boosted my confidence and spirit. I collaborated with Dr. Izdihar Jamil, Ph.D., and co-created a unique *TEDx* mastermind for women. Our goal is to help as many women as we can to become confident *TEDx* Speakers faster than they thought possible. We walk our clients through the methods, formulas, and tips we have created to help women become *TEDx* Speakers within a span of six to 12 months.

Grab the Opportunity

To find out more about the program, please send me an email at:
michelle@michellemehta.com
...with the Subject Line "TEDx Mastermind."

Power Summary

1. Say YES! when you really want something in your life.
2. Do NOT be afraid to step out of your comfort zone, even if it is scary.
3. Do NOT give up on your vision even if the world says NO!

Success Actions

1. Write down the reasons behind "WHY" you want to achieve a goal.
2. Write down the result of the goal you want to achieve.
3. Now FEEL it, Let EVERY bone in your body FEEL it. Think about how amazing this FEELS. Use ALL your five senses to make it GRAND and make it ALIVE. VISUALIZE it twice a day and watch the goal unfold.

*"Your heart will always lead the way to find
the power within you."*
~ Michelle Mehta

Best Wishes,

Michelle Mehta

Michelle Mehta

About the Author

Michelle Mehta is a *TEDx* Speaker, Confidence Expert, and International Bestselling Author. You may have seen her on the *Tonight Show* with Jay Leno, or interviewing people like Dr. Deepak Chopra and Vincente Fox, the former President of Mexico. ABC television said of Michelle, "She has overcome unthinkable obstacles and is one of the most successful teen coaches in 2020." Yahoo Finance named her as one of "The top 11 female coaches to follow in 2021."

She has worked with organizations like Morgan Stanley, MassMutual, and Wells Fargo. She has coached mayors of major California cities, and celebrities like James Haven, Angelina Jolie's brother.

Michelle speaks to teens and women all over the country about overcoming peer pressure, bullying, and low self-worth by increasing their confidence to live a life they fully love and admire themselves every single day.

She will even be sharing this message soon at the US Air Force Academy.

Grab the Opportunity

Contacts

Website: www.michellemehta.com

Email: michelle@michellemehta.com

> Free Consultation to discover if the *TEDx* Platform is right for you to grow your business. Please visit: https://calendly.com/michellemehta/tedx to book your free consultation.

Social Media

Facebook: www.facebook.com/iammichellemehta

LinkedIn: www.linkedin.com/in/iammichellemehta/

Instagram: www.instagram.com/iammichellemehta/

Focus and Imagination Create Results

Monica Ward, R.M.T., C.M.I.
Energy Healer, Transformational and High-Performance Coach, USA

*"When we suffer loss, we make space for
things even better than we imagined."*
~ Monica Ward

This Is Not a Drill

One of my biggest fears was experiencing a house fire in the middle of the night. Little did I know our dinner conversation that day was a prelude to one of the most eventful nights of my life, a night that led to devastating loss, human kindness, acceptance, determination, and perseverance.

It was a typical mid-January day. The Seattle sky was pouring down buckets of rain, kissing the ground with its sweetness, giving the beautiful lush, green terrain its daily drink of water.

My parents were over for Wednesday night dinner, allowing us time to stay connected. During dinner, my youngest, Mimi, asked me what we would do if our house burned down. Being an optimist, I told her we would probably move into the beautiful new apartments down the street. I didn't speak about our belongings being damaged; I didn't think about the animals we might lose; I didn't consider the PTSD we would all share for years to come.

Later that night, Mimi and I were brushing our teeth in my bathroom, and we noticed an unusual scent that smelled very familiar but was completely out of place. The bathroom was suddenly permeated with the smell like the inside of an oven does when you are heating it up to add some goodies to cook, and you open the oven door to the pungent smell of hot metal wafts up and infuses your nostrils. I went downstairs to check the oven, and it wasn't on.

While making my rounds to tuck the kids in, Mimi asked if she could sleep with me. This was a common event for us. She grabbed her favorite stuffed animals, and we went to my bed to drift off to a heavy sleep.

The fire alarm blared, pulling me out of bed. The continual, deafening "Beep! Beep! Beep!" … then a two-second pause … then "Beep! Beep! Beep!" … The pattern continued, and I could smell smoke. I ran to the closet and grabbed Mimi's robe. She jumped out of bed with her stuffed animals in tow, and we ran to my oldest daughter, Alexis' room, finding her still fast asleep with the blaring alarms going off. I shook Alexis, saying, "This is not a drill!" and we all ran downstairs.

Running out of the house, I was calling 911. The operator asked me if there was really a fire. She asked me to go back inside to check for smoke. Half asleep and pumping with adrenaline, I ran back up the stairs and stopped dead in my tracks. As my eyes darted around looking for fire, I suddenly had the most surreal, calm feeling. I saw soot hanging in the air all around me, like black snowflakes suspended in time. It was beautiful. I reached my hand out to see if my eyes were deceiving me and then noticed billows of grey smoke showing through the windows.

I ran back outside. It was still raining, and while making sure the girls had what they needed, I had forgotten to put something on my feet. Standing in the driveway barefoot, I recommended we all get into the Mini Cooper, out of the rain, and drive out of the way for the fire truck to come. We got into the car, but it wouldn't start. Not because the car itself was faulty, but because in the frenzy of adrenaline, I couldn't remember how to start the car. I kept pressing the "Push to Start" button, but the car would not start. Alexis calmly told me to put my foot on the clutch and then push the button, and as I followed her directions. The car started! We drove across the street and waited for the firemen.

As we were sitting there, we watched the house begin to blaze. The roof right above Mimi's bedroom window began to bubble up. It was expanding from the heat and formed a big bubble, then "BOOM!" it exploded with fire. Her room was completely engulfed in flames.

In a short time, the police arrived and then the firemen. We were told we had to stay and wait until the fire was mostly resolved. At 3 a.m., after the fire was completely extinguished, I went into the house to retrieve anything that might be salvageable. I grabbed some Converse, a pair of jeans, and undergarments, but I couldn't find any socks.

I had to try to secure an apartment the next day. While walking around in shoes with no socks, and a huge blister formed. The burning of the blister on my ankle rubbing on my shoe with every step I took was a reminder of the loss and total devastation we had just been through.

Focus and Imagination Create Results

The Undeniable Truth

That fire changed my life. I became hard, maybe even bitter, without knowing it. When it happened, I refused to let anyone know we were affected. I had Mimi go to her basketball game the next day, and she didn't miss a beat. My kids went to school, and I told them that, "These things happen. We are alive, and we can't stop to be sad for ourselves. We are blessed to have each other and have made it out alive."

Alexis wore her friend's clothes to school that week. When we were able to salvage some of her clothes, they had holes and burn marks on them, but she wore them like a badge of honor. People would remark on the condition of her clothes, and she would say, "Yeah, my house burned down, and this is what I have to wear," in a very matter-of-fact way.

My kids lost everything in their rooms. We moved into an apartment with mattresses on the floor. I don't recall if we had sheets or blankets the first night. I remember waking the first day in the apartment, and after taking a shower, I realized I didn't have a towel. Mimi was getting ready for school and didn't have a belt to keep her pants up. It's in these moments that you know how fortunate you have been.

The news about the fire had gotten out at work, and I found an outpouring of kindness. I was given a Target gift card and was able to buy the bedding, towels, and some essentials that we needed. I am not one to ask for help. This was so needed, I accepted it with overwhelming gratitude. People had really stepped up, people that didn't even know me. That kindness chipped away at my heart, softening me back up a bit.

I had been living paycheck to paycheck, and while we lost a beautiful rental house full of stuff, being in an empty apartment was sort of liberating. This allowed me to start from scratch and begin to create the reality I wanted to see. I had to show my girls that life doesn't stop here. This is an opportunity for a clean slate to manifest the life I really wanted.

I fetched a spiral notebook and pen I had purchased at Target and sat quietly.

Imagination Will Set You Free

Putting pen to paper, I sat down and emptied my mind, then asked myself, *What does a day in my ultimate life look like?*

I started visualizing, and after an hour, I had the most exquisite day written out. Without any judgment, I wrote out the absolute best day in my life. I wrote out exactly what I looked like, my healthiest, fittest body. I wrote out what I felt like when I woke, the beautiful view of the water from my bedroom window. I wrote out having coffee on the terrace, smelling the crisp Pacific Northwest morning air. I wrote out opening my banking app to see

$65K in savings, and so on until I had a full and complete day. I then read that writing at least twice a day, visualizing the entire day, step by step, using my senses to feel, touch, taste, and smell the events I was seeing in my mind. I became emotionally attached to the visualization.

I found myself spending my free time looking at homes for sale online that would seem absurdly out of my reach. Looking at the pictures of the houses, I would put myself them, looking out the windows, cooking in the kitchen, having cocktails on the patio with friends, falling asleep to the warmth of the fireplace crackling in the bedroom. I started listening to 528hz binaural beats videos to raise my vibration and noticed a remarkable difference in my attitude.

Something I should probably mention is that I have always had the ability to see and manipulate energy. It started as a kid, playing with the strands of light that I could see between my fingers while laying in bed at night, to eventually seeing energy vibrating and encompassing everything around me. I see the connectedness in all things, and because of this, I inherently understand the Law of Vibration and know for a fact that everything you could ever want or need is already there waiting for you to connect with it.

I kept up with the rituals I created, reading the ultimate day in my life, visualizing, and then started incorporating statements like, "I am so happy and grateful now that…" always writing in the present tense. I would read these statements every day, and soon I landed a job paying more than I had ever made. I bought a house, bought several cars, went on vacations, donated money, blankets, and gloves…I had created the life of my dreams.

Now I'm teaching others how to do the same.

Universal Laws

One of the biggest lessons I've learned is that we all must go through hardships. Without contrast, nothing can be understood. Without darkness, you can't know light. God's nature is Peace, Oneness, Love. Without contrast, without the illusion of Fear and Separation, we wouldn't have a contrasting mirror image to know Love and Oneness. God has given us the absolute and eternal Universal Laws, and they are here for everyone to tap into to help create the best experience. There are seven Universal Laws. The first three, the most important, cannot be changed.

The Three Immutable Higher Laws:

1. The Law of Mentalism (All Energy and Matter are created through the Mind);

2. The Law of Correspondence (As Above, So Below);
3. The Law of Vibration (Nothing rests. Everything is made of Vibrating Energy).

These laws were true for everyone, for every time, throughout creation. They never change. Every experience you've ever had is some combination of these laws. Once you understand with clarity these laws, you can create the reality you prefer.

You must think of your reality as something not outside of you. Think of it similarly to your reflection in the mirror. You know that you are not over there in the mirror; you are here. If you want to change that reflection in the mirror, you must change yourself, and then the reflection will change.

Physical reality, being a reflection, operates in the same type of fashion. Any change you want to see in your reality begins within. It's all based on your state of being. What you believe in your consciousness to be true for you is what is reflected in your reality. It's all based on consciousness; it's all based on vibration; it's all based on resonance; it's all based on state of being. Circumstances do not matter; only your state of being matters.

Your state of being creates your circumstances.

Me, an Entrepreneur?

While I have many certifications now, I am a high school dropout, continually told I wouldn't go anywhere in life. My dive into entrepreneurship began when I had my first child, Alexis. Her nervous system wasn't fully developed, and she needed to be massaged daily. I created a product line for mommies and babies called "Storks Kiss." Through sheer determination, I had it selling in many spas, baby stores, cosmetics stores and natural food stores. I remember sitting on a plane on my way to a personal appearance in Scottsdale, and the person sitting next to me asked me what I did for a living. When I told her, she asked me how in the world I was able to do this. I stopped for a minute to think. I realized I didn't know any different. I didn't know that I could fail. I just knew that my daughter needed a massage oil that didn't include toxins. I knew I had a passion for motherhood. I had such a love for this line I created I could easily share the information. Selling it came naturally.

Anyone can do anything. It's a matter of not having biases, not having judgment, being an empty vessel open to possibilities. The only element that can guarantee business success is the person driving the business. It's only when you stop limiting yourself with beliefs that your business can experience what you want. Give value. Give so much value that no one else around you makes sense. Give them a magical experience.

Losing Everything to Find Myself

When I look back, I realize that the moment I took the time to find clarity on what I really wanted my life to look like, I sparked my imagination, which in turn, started an avalanche of possibilities.

Here are some key things I've learned along the way.

Lesson 1: What you see when you look in the mirror is not the real you. It's just a reflection of your physical being. Our body is an instrument of the mind. Repetition fixes the idea in the subconscious mind. Thinking by itself will not change results. You must internalize the thinking. Creating repetition, the paradigm is changed, the behavior changes, and the results change.

Lesson 2: While your physical body and appearance are important, it's the self-image that's locked in your subconscious mind that really counts. This is the image that determines your success or failure in life.

Lesson 3: The real YOU is perfect, boundless, always looking for ways to expand. The self-image in your mind is based on false and limited information that sets the boundaries for every area of your life. You must change your self-image to fit what you want to see.

The Fruits of Daydreaming

The Universal Laws are available to everyone. We are all the same. We all have the same potential, similar desires, wants, and needs. We all hold all that potential within us. We don't have to call out to have these things come to us; they are already right there, waiting to be manifested. We ARE abundance. You don't have to learn how to manifest. This is automatic. It is built into you. You simply must manifest what you prefer rather than manifesting your unconscious beliefs.

One of the results of getting rid of limiting beliefs and acting on your passion is the increase of synchronicities.

Map out your life and live in your highest joy! In doing this, I'm now a #1 Best-Selling Author with the book _She Made It Happen_. I've written articles for "Explore! For the Professional" magazine, I'm considered an expert creator with featured posts on _LinkedIn_. I will be doing additional magazines and podcasts soon and have been invited to discuss an article in _Forbes_ magazine.

I can help you to figure out what you want your life to look like, and I can help you make it happen. **Click to book a call here:** **Free 1:1 Consultation**

Focus and Imagination Create Results

"I had the pleasure of working with Monica. Extremely knowledgeable, customer service driven, motivated for success, teacher, coach...just a few words to describe her. Monica's professionalism, communication, and creativity are huge differentiators and set her apart from the many trying to equal her success. She's a true student of her craft, and her expertise reflects significant depth and breadth, making her invaluable to those working with her and for her. I strongly endorse Monica and would welcome the opportunity to work with her again."
~ Wayde Stephens, VP of Sales/Business Development

Power Summary

1. Your circumstances do not dictate your future.
2. Paradigms are programmed through repetition.
3. We don't have to call out to have these things come to us; they are already right there, waiting to be manifested.

Success Actions

Here are three actions that you can do to help you change your life:

1. **Decide** – Know what you want. Sit quietly, forget all you know to be true. Craft your most amazing life without biases or judgment.
2. **Visualize** – Use your five senses to truly put yourself there, connect with it emotionally.
3. **Repetition** – Read it. Spend time visualizing every day, don't worry about "how" it will come to you.

"Your Reality and your Life are the product of what you Think about and what you Believe about your life."
~ Monica Ward

Much Love,

Monica Ward

About the Author

Monica Ward is a natural-born Energy Healer who has used these skills to become an inspirational Sales Leader. Her natural empathic skills have helped her to earn top recognition in her career year after year. Monica is a keynote speaker consulting on being an Empathic Energy Healer and using the Universal Laws to Manifest your Best Life.

Even as a child, Monica had a sense of the unlimited possibilities within human consciousness. Upon the realization that enlightenment is within all of us, she made the decision to tap into that force, to raise the vibration around her, and to continually attempt to help others to see their infinite potential.

Monica Ward

Contacts

Website: https://www.monicawardhealer.com/

LinkedIn: https://www.linkedin.com/in/monicaward/

Facebook: https://www.facebook.com/monicarward

Email: monicarward@gmail.com

The True Magic of Data Science

Nurfadhlina Mohd Sharef
Researcher in Data Science, Malaysia

For data to bring magic, it needs science,
leadership and governance.
~ Fadhlina

It's a team sport

"How many new cases today?"

R.I.P.

And then there were some condolence wishes... Then another new message came in... Then another... At least the later messages were not all black and white. But although the latest ones are on a map with red-amber-green color, they are not making things better. They are WARNINGS and MOURNINGS of how COVID19 has ripped people's life.

So there I was, thinking, "How could I play a role? How could I do better? How can we control this? When will the supply reach us? How many to distribute to Borneo?"

"Are your presentations ready?"

These are the questions that kept me bogged down for several weeks in January 2021. When other people got hunted with COVID19 cases.. I was busy facing a new phase of my life... On a mission to plan on how best to use data science to combat COVID19.

"Ladies and gentlemen, the vaccine supply distribution plan depends on the population statistics and the vaccine delivery schedule. The slide shows the completion target for each state based on 8 hours daily operation estimated based on 4 minutes jab per person. The average number of vaccination centre is shown in the dashboard, and the workforce expected is marked at the bottom." This presentation has set data science and data

113

governance to be the main strategy for vaccination management.

It's possible that statistics bore some people, but for me, its ability to unveil mystery keeps me going back for more adventure. I have used the statistics as descriptive and diagnostics analytics strategy to propose the plan for vaccine distribution. I lead a team of data scientists under the Academy of Sciences (ASM) that consists of an ensemble of researchers and professionals in academic and industrial backgrounds.

Data science is an intersection of statistics, visualization, and machine learning. Because statistics allows us to characterise the implicit patterns woven to resemble specific occurrences, this is possible. As a researcher in artificial intelligence (AI), knowledge and skills about machine learning is also a must. This is another common yet crucial approach to decode the data fingerprint beyond statistics' ability on data distributional pattern. To me, numbers are like riddles, and we can dive into the secret and unearth the story to understand what had transpired, as this could offer solutions to move forward.

I remember the time when I learned my first Python code about 6 years ago. I hooked up with a company that trains Python and had eventually become their official Academic Advisor. I was heavily pregnant at that time, so my main motivation was to prepare the twins for the envisioned digital life that awaits them. (I still recall my craze of playing dominos in a previous pregnancy because I want to train my first daughter to be a strategist). There were many interesting educational tools that came up along the way, and my daughter also had eventually completed several certificates for the young coder.

Fast-forward several years, I see that AI, machine learning, and data science are still indeed the most sought-after transformational strategies in many organisations, and "data is the new gold" was coined because of this phenomenon. Python is beginning to be taught at schools, and many non-coding-based data sciences are now available. Data are used to better define actions that are efficient, effective, and insightful. As a result, we were able to tell the difference between the regular and the anomalous data sets as a way of increasing productivity. Insights may also bring good (or bad) surprises. For example, in one of my consultation projects, the management was pleased that the insights from the data science eventually highlighted much good impact that the organisation has brought. But I had also used data science to discover some discrepancies in the data and operations that the organisation has handled. This became a vital eye-opener for the operational unit in that organisation and had eventually become one of the standard operating procedures.

The True Magic of Data Science

For the sake of futureproofing, many organisations begin an applied data science project by diving into algorithms and data before determining intended outcomes. Often, organisations are aware that they need data science capabilities, but they don't know where to begin. However, many neglects that an organisation's broader operations and strategic goals must guide the development of a data science strategy.

In fact, to begin any data strategy, the person in charge must first establish the organisation's strategic goals and identify chances for data science-based transformation. This is where I grew my experience in data science. Data science is a team sport comprising of a formal orchestration of people, processes, and technology. There must be an assorted cast of characters in a successful AI and data science transformation such as decision-maker, ethicist, ML/AI engineer, analyst, qualitative expert, economist, psychologist, reliability engineer, AI researcher, domain expert, UX specialist, statistician, and AI control theorist. I am fortunate to have been involved in several data science projects for several organisations in Malaysia in advisory, analyst, and scientist roles.

Data science governance is not stand-alone. I still remember the advice passed by a subject matter expert on a project. He is not from a computer science background. He said: "You are learning fast, but you may have worked too long with the computer". This challenge was the turning point for me better my communication. Yet, the learning curve for a data scientist, in my opinion, will never end. There will always be new algorithms, techniques, tools, and languages to learn on top of the new subject area. In spite of their greater experience, I believe that even the most experienced practitioners have been mesmerised by the gain of new findings. I'd like to share a similar story with you today.

Orchestrating data trajectory as a governance reform

"The data contains sensitive information. We need to collect the data first according to the format you suggest and discuss first before giving permission to access this data."

I think many would agree with me on how some people are so cautious with the data that their organisation "owns". Partly maybe because of the culture of being audited, hence being prudent, but even it is not easy to hurdle data from traditional ownership believes, success and truth usually speak for themselves. There is no one-size-fits all, but we can gain people's trust when we solve critical and relevant problems based on collaborative strategy and shared data. To encounter this, I usually request a small sample of data and offer to help clean and visualize their data. When I share the dashboard based on the analysis of obtained data, I highlight the potentially unexpected and unrealized things so they would be aware that this data trajectory control could leap into a governance reform. I learn that we can be persuasive, but we must show that we are trustworthy to persevere the situation.

Many senior executives possess the know-how tradition, but when some extraordinary happens, it typically is translated as anomalies and discarded, while this could be a hint of new values. Some projection tools are available, but data science, especially with machine learning, allows much richer decision making such as prediction ability by integrating complex data for pattern modelling. Once the hard ice between the project owner and the consultancy team had melted, the deer finally came into the open. I've found that the project owner or reps will eventually reveal more specifically about the areas where they require guidance which became the key to the success of the consultation projects. This is where the AI data products must also intuitively meet the users, and not necessarily those with sophisticated looks is the best. I enjoy learning client responses and experiment how information content, colours, and even layout play an impact to convey imperative messages.

In many apps nowadays dashboard is considered a standard mandatory feature. It offers convenience because the product utilizes data gathered about its user. This understanding makes it become assistive and addictive; it tells the reality to the user and shows how much they are understood by intelligently turning the data power to things that may please them. There is even a quote that says, "Data that is loved tends to survive," said Kurt Bollacker, a computer expert. Many people rely on automation, especially recommendation-based apps such as *Netflix, Spotify, Waze, Uber, Grab, Instagram,* and *TikTok*, which are all popular today. You can bet that it's not a comprehensive list.

Life-changing magic of data governance

"What is the risk if the new supply does not reach us by next week? Do we have enough stock now to meet our target?"

Sometimes this stomach-knotting sends chills down my spine. The reality on how there are a lot of unsung heroes behind the scenes playing the game of chances. These data scientists, logistics experts, epidemiologists, and pharmacists collectively strategizing plans to crunch the COVID-19 clusters. Having volunteers are also a blessing and maintains people bonding. Data science for COVID19 management is indeed a historic and massive data governance transformation globally. Imagine if we don't have apps to inform us of the status of cases around us?!

Rapid vaccine rollouts over the world and their potential impacts on transmission and mortality would influence public attitudes toward immunizations, reduce vaccine hesitancy, and, ultimately, contribute to an effective response to the pandemic. Malaysia targets 80% herd immunity about nearly 26 million people.

At the early stage of the National Immunisation Program, there are many meetings to consider various possible scenarios to firm up regulations and SOPs. The team combo developed calculators, simulators, and dashboards to estimate and project so everyone, regardless of nationality, age, location, or health condition, will be covered.

Many vaccines throughput models have been established to optimise the vaccination delivery schedule using statistics, heuristics, and machine learning algorithms. One of the approaches is on state daily vaccination throughput based on vaccine supply records, target population, the availability of VACs, and the vaccine completion target. Excel, PowerBI, Tableau, Python, and Google are some of the tools utilised to construct the solutions. There were also shocking and sad moments to hear people quarrel in the meeting mostly due to their frustration of this prolonged war and resulted to some of them easily flinched on a small matter.

"It's good that it will minimize contact but think about the cold chain. Malaysia is very hot, and there is also heavy rain. Setting up a drive-through would cost much. Imagine the traffic congestion that will cook up."

These are the typical comments and arguments when an agenda of new initiatives is being discussed. Decision-makers debate from various perspectives to imagine the implications from as little as parking space and layout to the vaccine throughput daily strategy. A drive-through vaccination administration centre (VAC) has eventually been one of the key implementations to reach the goal of vaccine throughput. The implications of the workforce and work plans have finally been managed properly.

The ASM team has also been assigned to develop the SOP/Guideline for Drive-through and Mobile VAC, SOP for Ventilation at VAC, and the SOP for setting up VAC at a house of worship (e.g. mosque and church). This initiative was set up in collaboration with national agencies such as National Security Council, the Ministry of Defence, the Department of Safety and Health, and several other relevant agencies. More than a few more innovations have then mushroomed, such as "pop-up" and outreach VAC, which extends the vaccine mobility. My experience engaging with National Heart Institute, Ministry of Health, Ministry of Science, Technology, and Innovation, and several other stakeholders nationwide told me various professional perspectives pour their efforts inseparably in harmony for our survival against the pandemic.

"We offer four units of refurbished trucks to operate as mobile VAC for aborigines. Our setup complies with the ventilation requirements and is disabled-friendly. Our team consists of our in-house medical unit and volunteers with our in-house ambulance."

This is real... There truly exists such generous, idealistic, and inspiring organisation which fight in this war with brevity and caring to save people's lives. I met these kind of people because ASM has also been tasked to chair a technical approval committee for the opening of a drive-through and mobile VAC. I saw various kinds of mischievous businessmen also as some try to take financial advantage because of misunderstanding that the vaccination administration setup commission can be turned as a profit-making exercise. There are also associations that genuinely come up with pure vaccination protection programs as front liners and supporting plain goodwill. Lucky there are still many genuinely impressive and kind-hearted people who go humanity first despite their social status. A thorough data science leadership and governance have indeed held an impact in ensuring a well-coordinated COVID-19 vaccination administration and management handling to achieve its target.

Data science leadership may not teach us how to add happiness or how to minus sadness, but it does teach us one vital thing... that every problem has a solution. In Islam, leadership is a *fard kifayah*, which is a collective duty upon Muslims, the discharge of which by some of them absolves the rest of its performance. Leadership in Islam is rooted in belief and willing submission to the Creator, Allah. Prophet Muhammad (PBUH) taught that a leader is not the one who everyone else serves, but the one who serves and betters his/her people. His prophetic leadership qualities of integrity and trust, vision, courage, competence, fairness, decisiveness, wisdom, patience, compassion and warmth, emotional and spiritual intelligence and servant-leadership, compel me to reflect on my own actions and to constantly strive for betterment.

"It is never wrong to do the right thing"
(by Mark Twain)

The finest reward of being a researcher or academician in my line of work is having creative freedom. Even though many of my species' moan about the overburdening KPIs and demands for us to morph (fantastically) beneath a variety of hats, I still value our relatively flat organisational hierarchy in comparison to the multi-hierarchy structure. Because of this, we can flourish in a way that is not too loose yet secure enough for us to grow. When compared to the typical teaching-supervision-researcher-writer positions, those who want to be proactive and imaginative by exploring and contributing to initiatives may find themselves perpetually busy. However, the enormous strain we are under indicates that our dedication and hard work are paying off.

Take a look at these notable quotes...

*"The first three letters of success are
TRY."*
~ John T. Matsik

*"Your future is created by what you do
today, not tomorrow."*
~ Robert Kiyosaki

*"Life is like riding a bicycle. To keep your
balance, you must keep moving."*
~Robert Einstein)

Which one is your favourite? Or do you have anything else in mind?

All of the above are favourites of mine, but I'd like to dedicate the following quote to you:

"Success is judged by how high you bounce when you reach rock bottom."

I love this statement because it inspires us to rebuild ourselves by focusing on our strengths instead of comparing ourselves to other people.

My point is that life should be worth loving rather than just living, and this may mean doing things extraordinarily and disruptively. Sometimes it is difficult to change from some comfort zone especially as the move will make us deter from our convenient old-school. But we can sense that we are static when we see our competitive evolving much farther than us. This is similar to setting up a transformation in our organisation or catalysing it. Each of us plays a role!

Having data science framework as a newly formed policy in the organisation will warrant refining scientific practices around data acumen as well as shift from the typical job literacy. As the industry races to harness the power of data, demand for quality data insights is growing at an increasing rate. Designing data governance that delivers value is imperative for a healthy organisation. Without quality-assuring governance, companies will not only miss out on data-driven opportunities but will also waste resources. According to Cassie Kozyrkov, the Chief Decision Data Scientist at Google, there are five steps for a successful data science transformation:

1. Figure out who's in charge (appoint a benevolent dictator).
2. Identify the use case and focus on the outputs.

3. Do some reality checks - do you have the data? Do you have suitable machines?
4. Assemble your team, with correct human capital and skillsets.

Craft a business performance metric wisely and set the testing criteria to overcome human biases.

Thus, being useful and resourceful, similar to a human, are two contemporary techniques essential to living in our period. Some survival tips from me:

a) Be in surroundings that will inspire and excite you, those that provide valuable opportunities to keep your thrill.
b) Get mentors and engage with others while supporting and protecting each other.

Sadness is a natural human reaction at various times of life. When you're unhappy or depressed for no apparent reason, take a few deep breaths and look for ways to find joy, such as exercising, watching a favourite show, playing a game, eating something healthy and comforting, and being in the company of loved ones. The most basic thing you can do is read something inspiring. You can keep doing what you're doing, which means you'll keep feeling unsatisfactory. You may either make a change or try to get back on your feet. Seek competent advice as quickly as possible, and always believe in yourself.

Remember that life is a gift, and it is extremely valuable! May you be filled with kindness, joy, love, happiness, and abundance throughout your life.

So here are some key actions for you:

Remember, "It always is impossible until it's done" (Nelson Mendela), so choose the best areas for early-stage development and understand how to scale data science solutions.

Love and blessings,

fadlh

Nurfadhlina Mohd Sharef

About the Author

Nurfadhlina Mohd Sharef is an Associate Professor at the Faculty of Computer Science and Information Technology, Universiti Putra Malaysia, Malaysia and is currently serving as the Deputy Director (Innovation in Teaching and Learning) at the Centre for Academic Development (CADe) in UPM. She is also active in the Young Scientists Network-Academy of Sciences Malaysia and a member of the National Council of e-Learning for Public Universities. Dr. Fadhlina's main research interest is in data science and intelligent computing. She has also been active in eLearning projects.

Her consultancy projects revolve around data science for public and private agencies. She is usually assigned to teach courses related to Artificial Intelligence. In her teaching, she usually emphasizes on experiential learning and believes blended learning is the best method to learn and teach.

She loves seeing seeds that she planted sprouts, grow into greens and colors and eventually harvestable so daydreaming and gardening are her favorite pastimes. Her other hobbies are cooking besides reading and watching movies.

Nurfadhlina Mohd Sharef

Contacts

Email: nurfadhlina@upm.edu.my

Website: https://sites.google.com/view/nurfadhlina

LinkedIn: https://www.linkedin.com/in/nurfadhlina-mohd-sharef-89aaaa6/

Facebook: https://www.facebook.com/nurfadhlina.mohdsharef

Successful at Work, Struggling at Love

Solving the Professional Woman's Dating Dilemma

Raeeka Yaghmai
Love and Relationship Coach*, USA

> * Raeeka's expertise is in working with single straight women looking for single straight men. This chapter is written from that perspective, but it applies to everyone of any sexual orientation.

"Emotional Freedom happens when we lean into what we most fear."
~ Raeeka Yaghmai

He Broke Up with Me "Again"!

I was sobbing on the hallway floor of my San Francisco flat, begging my fiancé not to leave. I felt empty, lifeless. I could hardly breathe. I was in a heightened state of panic and fear and shifting into total survival mode. Anxiety had taken over my entire body and was holding me hostage. This was the second time my fiancé was pulling an act of disappearance from our relationship and leaving me drifting in his wake.

We were supposed to go to Los Angeles to spend the winter holidays with my family. My family was waiting for us, but all my sobbing, begging, and pleading with him didn't work. He left and moved out of our flat completely. The half-empty closets, drawers, shelves, and bed were like ghosts haunting me with a reminder that I was so lonely and left behind... *Again!*

And then a harsh reality hit me – I had to tell my family. My *family*?! They were expecting us in just a few days. How could I face them? What would my relatives and friends think? My big Persian community of friends and family had called months ago to congratulate me on our engagement. What would they think of me now?

And before I knew it, deep wounded thoughts that I had carried for years

123

and years, the secret demons, were out again to haunt me…

"What is wrong with me?"
"Why can't I keep a man?"
"I'm not enough for a man to love me."
"Why do men always leave me?"
"I'll end up alone for the rest of my life."
"What would everybody think of how I can't keep a man?"

Why couldn't a high-achieving, well-educated, highly sophisticated, and successful opera singer with an impressive resume such as myself manage to keep a man? I should know better. I was so frustrated.

I became obsessed with getting him back. It was my day job, night job, 24-hours-a-day job – *to get him back*. I went to six hours of therapy per week and accumulated over $10,000 of debt just to learn how to get my fiancé back. My livelihood depended on it. I couldn't and wouldn't rest until I had him back.

The saddest part was that not once did I ask myself, *Raeeka, what do you want in a relationship?* I was so twisted in my obsession to get him back that I had lost touch with knowing why I wanted him back.

This reaction of mine wasn't unprecedented. Before my fiancé, I had about 10 relationships end very similarly. All those men either cheated on me or disappeared. This could not be happening to me again. This time things *had* to be different.

My academic education was in vocal performance and opera. Opera is the "Olympics of singing," and I was trained to try things over and over until I got it, so I was doing exactly what I had learned. If I'd learned only one thing throughout my bachelor's, master's, and postgraduate degrees, it was to never, ever give up. But I was doing all this with the wrong man – although I succeeded, and he came back about four months later.

Emotional Freedom

Eleven months later, I was at the Apple store getting training on my new computer when I received a text: "Raeeka, please come home right now." I knew exactly what that meant!

He was leaving, *Again*!

But this time, I was ready. I couldn't believe how calm and centered I was. I wasn't the same person who was sobbing 11 months ago, paralyzed by the fear of losing him.

Successful at Work, Struggling at Love

A few months prior, I was sitting at the kitchen table studying for my life-coaching certification and learning about the different ways that we as humans show up in our lives. I remember that moment so distinctly. As I finished the chapter I was on, I put the book down on my lap and started asking myself questions that I had never asked before:

"What do I want to experience in my relationship?"
"What are my life aspirations?"
"What do I truly desire in my heart?"
"How aligned is my current relationship with my authentic self and true desires?"

My love life patterns and relationships played like a history documentary in my head, and as I was examining how every man with whom I'd had a romantic relationship had cheated on me, including my soon-to-be ex-fiancé, I had the most powerful realization:

"I am the common denominator between all my romantic relationships."

I started asking myself a series of what I call quality questions:

"Who do I need to be, and how do I need to show up to attract the right partner?"
"What are my love blind spots?"
"What causes me to accept the wrong man in my life?"
"How can I communicate my needs and set boundaries with ease?"

It was then that I realized that my academic education and knowledge and my success in my career have absolutely nothing to do with how to create a successful and healthy relationship.

I felt like I could finally breathe. I remember feeling unbelievably calm and grounded, knowing deep down that the relationship I'm in is my reaction to my past emotional wounds and pains. I knew at that moment that my fiancé was not the right man for me moving forward. At the same time, I felt so much compassion and gratitude towards him because I knew how much I had evolved in this relationship experience with him.

I couldn't believe myself smiling softly as I came to that realization and wondering if this feeling was a momentary thing and that it would pass...but it wasn't.

Little did I know that throughout the months of working on getting him back followed by completing my certification as a life coach, I was really

125

working on what I now call "Love Education."

Love Education

In the past, families and friends would play a big role in matching a couple. Many times, marriages served as keeping the financial and social power within the inner circle or by merging two families. There was not much of a choice in who we chose as our partners.

Relationships have changed a lot since then, not only from years ago, or the '40s, '50s, and '60s, but just in the last 15 to 20 years with the social media and smartphone boom. Add to the mix the rise of women's equality, independence, and empowerment that is opening space for women to rise to higher ranks and positions in the work area across the globe.

At the same time, divorce rates are continuously going up. Many people who find themselves in unhappy marriages are choosing to stay, either because of their children, financial limitations, or social/cultural pressure. Many successful, independent women are also choosing to stay single, but, at the same time, they suffer from loneliness, anxiety, and depression.

While women have gained more visibility and power in the work field, the roles of men and women have changed, and there is a global confusion around how to navigate our love life as the old ways of finding love are no longer working.

There are thousands, probably millions, of smart, strong, educated women with high-level careers wondering why they can't crack the code of their love life given their success.

But, there's hope! There are two basic reasons that are the root of our struggle in finding love. The good news? They are both very figure-out-able and changeable, and once you know what they are and where to start, finding love will become a much easier process!

What You Need to Know

1 – It's Time to Get Our Love Education

Our academic education doesn't teach us how to create a healthy love life. There is a huge misconception that having an academic education is enough for finding love.

It wasn't until my fiancé, who I thought was "the one" for me, broke my heart for the third time that I realized it's not the men; it's me. Not that there's anything wrong with me. It's simply that I have no education when it comes to how to date, how to choose my romantic partner, and how to navigate my romantic relationships. Like any successful, educated woman, I'd been trying to create my love life based on my academic education and information, which is like trying to fly a plane because we know how to drive a car.

In a world where the focus from a very young age is on school grades, higher education, and then finding a successful career that allows us to excel both financially and in rank, nobody taught us how to find the right life partner. There is no education around dating and romantic relationship navigation.

Bring into that mix the fact that many of us have not had parents who set healthy, happy relationships as examples of love. Many of us don't have role models that show us what a successful and passionate romantic relationship looks like. Many of us come from cultures where we are taught what should and shouldn't be done when it comes to finding love, but these teachings are in complete conflict with the women we have become after obtaining higher education, living in a different society than our culture, and becoming these amazing empowered and independent women.

This is why it's crucial that we educate ourselves on how to create a healthy, happy, and fulfilling love life. Like in our academic education where we obtain a blueprint and certain skillsets to eventually succeed in our careers, Love Education will provide the proper skillsets that will support us to succeed in love and prevent years of heartbreak, messy and expensive divorces, not to mention emotional, physical, or financial abuse.

2 – Ask for Help from the Right People

This is a big one. We live in a global culture where everybody and anybody considers themselves an expert in giving love advice. Would you go to your mortgage broker to get advice on your cholesterol level? Yet, that's what we do with our love life. We reach out to friends and family to ask for advice in our love life, but 99% of the time, they are not skilled in this area. They either suggest what worked for them, or worse, tell you what to avoid based on their own heartbreaking experiences.

It's time to give our love life the same level of respect, value, and importance that we give to all other areas of our lives. It's time to be brave and take pride in standing for love education. We need to recognize how deep the shame around not being able to figure out our love life is. From an early age, we are taught that we should be able to do it instinctively. In some cultures or families, we are shamed, ridiculed, and labeled if we are single or decide to break up or get a divorce.

So on the one hand, we tell the world where we got our academic education by putting it in our bios, our resumes, our *LinkedIn* profiles, and on the other hand, we are so ashamed to ask for help or share that we are taking classes and educating ourselves in this area. We keep it super-confidential and don't want anyone to know, as if we are doing something terribly wrong.

Brene Brown says: "Shame needs three things to grow exponentially:

127

secrecy, silence, and judgment." If you remove these things, shame can't exist.

Imagine what would be possible to all of us in our love life if we considered Love Education a prestigious thing.

Unfortunately, without having Love Education, many repeat the old approaches that never worked in the past. And after years of experiencing the same unwanted results, we decide that finding love isn't in the cards for us, or dating doesn't work anymore, or that the days of finding the right match are gone. Before we know it, we are battling an internal conflict where our head knows our worth, and our heart is frustrated, disappointed, and ready to give up.

Sadly this all happens because the principle behind our approach to finding love never changes. It's like we are driving in a foreign country with no map, no GPS, with very little gas, hoping and praying we'll find a gas station.

What's Possible

To love and be loved is your birthright – like freedom. Every smart, educated, successful woman deserves to have both career success and enjoy a fulfilling partnership.

Imagine having the knowledge and tools to navigate your love life with ease and confidence. Imagine being able to set boundaries without feeling tightness around them. Imagine recognizing the red flags in the earlier stages and saving months and years from getting stuck in the wrong relationship. Imagine finding the man that would love you, support your dreams and mission, respect and admire you, and care for you. Imagine going through life with a true partner.

Imagine putting an end to emotional, physical, and sexual abuse by educating ourselves on love and relationships, having the same trust we have in our career success to thrive in this area of our lives. Imagine feeling so confident to be able to say STOP! or NO! to the wrong match and the wrong relationship.

Our love life is the most vulnerable part of our life. Healthy love is like oxygen for our heart. When our love life is going well, when our heart and soul is safe and thriving, the rest of our life follows.

You CAN have all of that when you have Love Education!

Power Summary

Let's recap some of the key points in this chapter:

Successful at Work, Struggling at Love

1. Our academic education has not prepared us for succeeding in our love life. It is time to value our love life and invest in our Love Education to fill the gap between our career success and love-life success.
2. I am the common denominator between all my romantic relationships. If I change my ways, my relationships can change.
3. In the era of women's empowerment, it is crucial to have our Love Education to be able to navigate the appropriate energies between our career and love life.

Success Actions

Here is an easy step you can take right away to start your #LoveEducation process. I LOVE connecting with high-performing, smart women like you. Reach out and tell me:

- What would excite you the most to see in your love life in the next 6 months?

I look forward to hearing from you!

Love,

Raeeka

"The quality of your questions determines the quality of your life and love life."
~Raeeka Yaghmai

About the Author

Raeeka Yaghmai is an award-winning dating blogger, host of the *DWC-TV*, and the founder and CEO of Dating with Confidence™. Known for her unique "Lasting Love Method," she helps single, high-performing women from around the world discover their love blind spots so they can stop attracting the wrong men and find love with their ideal partner in a way that feels authentic and empowering to them, even if they don't know where to look.

Her approachable, compassionate, and warm personality, along with her vast knowledge of modern dating and relationships, combines with her powerful coaching ability to make her a unique and highly sought-after mentor.

In addition to working with women from all over the globe, her unique perspective as an Iranian American has made her a go-to dating coach for professional female immigrants navigating the Western dating world.

Raeeka is an advocate of education for dating and relationships, which is strongly missing from the traditional academic system as well as women empowerment. Having gone through numerous heartbreaks and years of struggle with finding love, she understands firsthand how frustrating, lonely, and confusing dating and finding love can be.

Successful at Work, Struggling at Love

Coaching highly driven, successful women for over a decade and seeing them all struggle with the same things when it comes to dating and finding love, she is passionately committed to putting an end to their struggle in this area of their lives and helping them make one of the most important decisions of their lives with clarity, courage, and confidence.

She's been featured in *Your Tango, Blog Talk Radio, Nourishing Real Talk, K.I.R.N. 670 AM Radio, Guy's Guy Radio, Bustle, Elite Daily, The Bright Side of Life*, and *Learn It Live*.

Contacts

Website: www.DatingWithConfidenceCoaching.com

Email: raeeka@DatingWithConfidenceCoaching.com

Facebook Messenger: https://m.me/raeeka.shehabiyaghmai

> The "Broken Picker" Solution goes into detail about how to avoid unavailable guys and identify the right relationship-ready men with actionable steps you can implement right away and before you go on another date!
> **Free Training:**
> https://datingwithconfidencecoaching.com/bps

> Join our Free *Facebook* group "Dating with Confidence for The Successful Professional Woman" to get access to exclusive members-only Love Education resources.
> *Facebook:*
> https://datingwithconfidencecoaching.com/fbgroup

LinkedIn: https://www.linkedin.com/in/datingwithconfidence

Instagram: https://www.instagram.com/datingwithconfidence

Podcast: https://datingwithconfidencecoaching.com/podcast/

A Foundation of Confidence

Sara M. Ruda
Speaker/Coach, USA

"I choose to live by choice, not by chance."
~ Sara Ruda

It Falls Apart

"I can't believe you were actually able to do something like that!"

"That's not the person I know."

These were not the responses I had expected when I began telling people I had become a published author – and an International Bestseller at that. I had been trying for years to get my writing in order to become a published author, and it had finally happened! I was humbled, proud, exhausted, and relieved. I wanted to shout to the world the accomplishment of my long-lived dream come true.

Those closest to me knew how hard I had worked for this moment and how important it was to me. When I began telling others, I was met with remarks about being shocked that I was able to do such a thing and that they didn't think I was capable of it. Others said that it didn't sound like I was the person they knew to be able to accomplish this kind of task. I didn't let my feelings of hurt and disappointment show, and at the time, I just laughed it off and told them to expect even more from me.

I began to second guess if I was really ready to be at this level. I knew I wanted to be an author. I knew I wanted to be able to help people and inspire people. I know I am a motivated, hardworking, good person. What did they see that I didn't? What prompted those kinds of responses?

As I reflected on these questions, I started to ask myself other questions as well. How well do these people really know me? Are they really invested

133

in my well-being? Do they even care if I succeed?

Along with this, I came to the realization that I am now on an international platform and open to negative comments 24/7. Of course, I was aware of this. I have Facebook and watch what happens on TV and see the media. But, I had not taken the time to come to terms with the reality of it in my personal life.

I work in pre-hospital medicine, and I am very familiar with people being upset and sometimes saying untoward things to me and my partner, which I know to never take personally. But this felt very different and was hard to let "roll off," even though the people making the comments knew just as much about me as some of the people I talk to for 10 minutes during a transport.

Why did their opinion matter so much to me? That was the big question…

The Turning Point

That's when I had my revelation. My journey is exactly that – MINE. Opinions are a dime a dozen, and as long as I knew I was following my path and doing what I knew was right for me, then I would be able to remain confident and achieve my goals. What had initially begun to inhibit my forward progress turned into motivation to not only continue on but to become the best at what I do. There would be no doubt that I deserve to be where I am regardless of what the critics said. I realized that there is a purpose for negative comments. Without them, there isn't that extra motivation to continue to get better.

I think inside, we all like to prove people wrong about our abilities and show that we can achieve more than what is believed. It can be exciting to overcome obstacles that were set not only by ourselves but by others as well. Success at anything always starts with how well you maintain your self-discipline and your ability to turn a negative event or situation into something positive for yourself. This has been my foundation for moving forward in every challenging situation.

The Impact

I was able to build a mindset where I knew that sometimes people will say negative things, and I am okay with that. I am okay with it because I know that what I am doing is more important than the negative things that they have to say. They don't have enough personal access to me for it to hold any real truth. Having this new thought process reinforced my confidence in what my purpose is and led me to pitch a book idea, and I am now curating my first multi-author book project. In addition to that, I continue to build my coaching business where I help women, children, and men recovering from traumatic events regain their self-confidence through experiencing and learning about the outdoors. I used the challenge presented to me as a chance to grow and improve myself as a leader.

The Hard Truth

I could have easily just given up and taken what those people said to heart and been done. Despite the amazing feat of becoming a bestselling author under my belt, I had still felt defeated and questioned myself!!! There will always be doubters and critics to pick apart everything you do. As a leader and influencer, you must always remember that the only power they have is the power you give them.

At first, I had given my critics the power over me and was overcome with self-doubt, which challenged everything I had been working so hard to achieve. When I took the time to reflect, I couldn't believe that they weren't as happy as I was. But then, when I took a step back, I realized that they did not see all the work that went into it, they do not have the same goals, and we all have different ideas of what is important and different interests.

The important thing is not what other people think, but what you think – what YOUR goals are and what you want to achieve

My Real World

Having grown up in small towns despite moving as a military kid, I was able to be surrounded by caring and supportive communities. When we moved back to where I graduated high school and call my hometown in Nebraska, there was always motivation and constructive criticism of what you would do to help you become better. I also grew up to be independent and confident in my abilities to take care of whatever needs I may have.

Fast forward into college and the "real world." There was still motivation, but it became clear that not everyone was there to help me become a better version of myself, and it was more of a "me" environment. I quickly learned how to adapt to my surroundings and that I could not take everything personally. Despite this, I always went out of my way to try and help others, even if I did not know them. This led me into the medical field, and I fell in love with it.

I obtained my degree in paramedicine and loved the fact that I was able to help others in their time of need. In the medical field, especially pre-hospital, you learn to not take things that people say personally. They could be going through the worst experience of their life and will say things that they don't mean or don't even realize they're saying it. Even through this, I would find comfort in knowing that I could be there to help.

During this time, I became involved in an abusive relationship and was able to get back to the Midwest where my family resides, but not without letting my paramedic license lapse and losing everything I had owned. That experience inspired me to reach out to others who are also going through, or have been through, traumatic events and encourage them to not lose hope and that a better life is possible.

In my #1 Bestselling Book *Ambitious Women Rise*, I tell my story of escaping my abusive relationship and the hope of a new start.

> You can find that book at:
>
> https://www.lulu.com/en/us/shop/sara-ruda/ambitious-women-rise/paperback/product-zndy2w.html?page=1&pageSize=4

I now live in northwest Kansas with my husband and son on a ranch where I have been recertified in Emergency Medical Services. I am also a nurse and continue to help people during this time of COVID-19. I continue to build my coaching business, where I use exposure to the outdoors as a way to build self-confidence, and also do motivational speaking for groups.

My Lessons Learned

There will always be critics, and not everyone will like you or understand what you are trying to accomplish – and that's okay. It's not their job to understand your goals; it's yours and who you are trying to help and your clients. When I decided to shut out the critics, there was a newfound focus on what my plan was, and everything started to fall in place. We alone have the power to control our thoughts, and it is up to us to make sure we stay positive and motivated. With this mindset, I was able to become a bestselling author, a motivational speaker and start my unique Outdoor Coaching process.

Stay focused on your goal and your passion, ignore the critics, and only take the advice of those who want to see you succeed. There is always room for suggestions and constructive criticism but not for negativity. Surround yourself with those who lift you up, and make sure you are always your biggest fan!

A Foundation of Confidence

Takeaways

Takeaway #1 – Stay true to yourself! There will be times that you will be tempted to change your style or your ideas based on what someone says but do not falter from who you are. What you do now between your strong work ethic, how you work with people, and your business strategy and ideas are what will make you successful with your specific target audience.

Takeaway #2 – Your ability to turn negative events into positive outcomes relies heavily on your self-discipline and ability to stay focused on your goals and what you really want. We are human and make mistakes, have feelings, and need a break sometimes. Don't let a misstep or delay distract you from the big picture.

Takeaway #3 – Continue to build your self-confidence. How? Small things make a big difference. Make small promises to yourself and keep them. Set small, attainable goals and achieve them. These small goals will be stepping stones to bigger goals. Do something nice and random for yourself and/or for someone else. Take the time to write down three things you like about yourself at least twice a week. Continuous positive reinforcement will help you to build confidence, and it will show in everything you do.

Takeaway #4 – Set your goal and know exactly what you want! Once you know what you want, then you can work on how to get there. You need to know where you are going before you start. This helps with your confidence because you can say with certainty what your goals are, and it shows your desire and that you have determined what your purpose is.

Rewards

I continue to build my business and pursue my passion, which is to help people, and I get to do that on an international level! This is all possible while having the time to spend with my family, and it allows me to be a good example to my son. He gets to see what it means to work hard for what you want and never give up. I encourage a positive mindset and show him that even though there may be temporary setbacks, it does not mean we stop pursuing our goals.

The ability to command my mindset has also led me to be featured on NBC, ABC, FOX, CBS, and *Business Innovator* magazine as an inspiring female entrepreneur. I have also been featured as an upcoming business to watch in *Small Business Trendsetters*.

I was able to free myself from my self-doubt, and when that happened, my business began to flourish. I was able to really put myself out there and be genuine with my cause without fear of judgment. It brought me to a whole different level of leadership because I am here to help others who have been in my position in the past. I can get them from where I was, and they are, to where I am now. I am a confident entrepreneur with my own business pursuing my passion.

What more can you ask for?

Power Summary/Recap

1. Why is self-discipline so important?

2. When should you set your goal?

3. What kind of people should you surround yourself with?

Doable Success Actions

1. Set a clear goal for yourself. What is your vision and purpose? This is the starting point and the foundation that sets you up for everything else that you will do moving forward. You have to know where you are going before you start.

2. Make a point to surround yourself with positive people who support your goals. Your group should also encourage you to stay positive during the difficult moments.

3. Take the time to boost your self-confidence. Write down three things you like about yourself, write down a promise to yourself and keep it. Do some extra self-care. All of this will help you become more motivated and increase your positive mindset.

A Foundation of Confidence

*"We alone decide how we react and what
we will do in challenging times. Use each
challenge as an opportunity to learn and
become even better at what you do."*
~ Sara Ruda

Always Move Forward!

Sara M. Ruda

About the Author

Sara M. Ruda is an International Bestselling Author, Motivational Speaker, and Coach who lives in northwest Kansas with her husband and son who farm and ranch. She also works in Prehospital Emergency Medicine as an Emergency Medical Technician.

Her main focus with her clients is to help them regroup, refocus, and reconnect with who they are by rebuilding self-confidence through learning about the outdoors. Outdoor coaching has a unique ability to help clients not only build up new abilities but allows them to detach from the chaos of the tech world and really focus on themselves. Her clients have had amazing results and new skills to use in their daily lives.

In her spare time, she enjoys reading with her son and going on family trips and adventures in Nebraska.

Contacts

Website: https://saramruda.com

Email: srmidwesthuntress@gmail.com

Free Gift!

30-Minute Coaching Session on Outdoor Activity via *Zoom*

srmidwesthuntress@gmail.com

Social Media

Stay connected with Ruda on *Facebook* @SaraRuttenMidwestHuntress
https://www.facebook.com/midwesthuntressKS

Instagram: @nebraskahuntress

Made in United States
Orlando, FL
07 April 2022